HOW TO COOL DOWN
WHEN THINGS
REALLY HEAT UP

A Practical Guide to Managing

Stress and Prioritizing

Self-Care

∾

MALCOLM ERIC MEADOWS

ISBN 979-8-218-89054-4

To My Wife

My "Main Thing" and the most resilient human I know.

With great respect, admiration, and love.

Table of Contents

Foreword

How to Cool Down When Things Really Heat Up, is a written reflection of a workshop I've delivered with enthusiastic irregularity for nearly two decades. What began in educational settings gradually expanded into corporate, government, and nonprofit spaces. Over the years, I've shared this material with groups ranging from a dozen participants to several hundred—in formats as brief as a single 90-minute session and as comprehensive as full-day programs. Whether presented as a standalone experience or part of a larger initiative, the heart of the message has remained the same: practical, thoughtful strategies for navigating stress, emotional fatigue, and the demands of daily life.

If you're reading this after attending the workshop, much of the content will feel familiar. The book offers additional components that expand on what we covered together: quotes and parables, reflection exercises, and suggestions for further reading. Of course, the live interaction and small-group activities bring a dynamic, human element that no book can fully replicate. But if you haven't attended the workshop, don't worry. This book stands on its own, and I hope you'll consider joining us in person someday to experience the full journey.

In *The Call of Stories*, Robert Coles explores the idea that listening to stories fosters learning and self-discovery. The stories shared in this book are all true, drawn from my experiences in education, the nonprofit sector, and government work as well as from my life as a husband, parent, and friend. When shared in live workshops, these stories consistently bring the material to life. Participants often tell me, even years later, that it was the stories they remembered most and that those stories helped the lessons stick.

The setting for my first story is Atlanta, on my very first day as an educator. I was teaching upper school economics. It was my very first class and my very first time in front of students. I wasn't nervous about the material; I just wanted to connect and make it meaningful. As the class ended and students began to leave, I noticed the Headmaster standing outside the door, casually greeting the seniors. I overheard him ask the last student, "And what did we learn today, Mr. Smith?" Without hesitation, the young man replied, "I don't know, but I know I want to do it again tomorrow." They both smiled. Then the Headmaster turned to me and said, "You've found your calling. You are a teacher."

I share that story for a reason. We all gather bits of wisdom from the books we read and the seminars we attend. But when you close *this* book, I don't want everything to be neatly resolved. In fact, I hope it leaves you a little unsettled. I hope that months from now, while driving to work or sitting quietly with your thoughts, something you read here resurfaces, something here finally connects with your life in a new way. Maybe it even brings a tear to your eye and makes you rethink your entire day. Because the goal isn't to solve every problem. That's not realistic. The goal is to live more peacefully with the questions and to carry with you the promise of a better tomorrow.

Introduction: You're Not Alone

Start where you are. Use what you have. Do what you can. (Ashe)

I'm not a celebrity. I'm not a guru. I'm not a genius with a dozen degrees on the wall. I'm just one of you...someone who's been through the fire, felt the heat, and learned how to cool down without burning out.

This book isn't about perfection. It's about progress. It's about learning how to take care of yourself when life feels like it's spinning out of control. It's about recognizing that emotional exhaustion, burnout, and stress are not signs of weakness; they are signals. And if we listen to them, they can guide us toward healing, growth, and resilience.

You'll find stories, strategies, and science here. You'll also find honesty. Because let's face it: sometimes life is hard. But that doesn't mean we have to go through it alone or without tools.

So, take a deep breath. You're here. You're ready. Let's begin.

What Is Stress, Really?

It's not stress that kills us, it is our reaction to it. (Selye)

Stress is a word we throw around a lot. "I'm so stressed." "This job is stressing me out." "I can't handle this stress." We even do "stress" tests to see if our heart is healthy! But what is it, really?

According to Hans Selye, an endocrinologist and pioneer in stress research, stress is "a non-specific response of the body to any demand placed upon it." That means stress isn't just about bad things. It's about change. It's about pressure. It's about anything that requires us to adapt. And once you understand what stress really is, you can begin to take back control.

There are two kinds of stress:

Eustress is often called "positive stress." It arises when pressure or challenge feels within our coping abilities and can lead to growth, motivation, and improved performance. Think about preparing for a job interview, training for a marathon, or planning a wedding. These events may be demanding, but they also bring excitement, purpose, and a sense of accomplishment. Eustress energizes us and helps us stay focused and engaged.

Distress is "negative stress" that occurs when demands exceed our perceived ability to cope. Losing a job, experiencing a breakup, dealing with chronic illness—these situations drain emotional and physical resources and can lead to burnout, depression, or other health issues if not managed properly. Distress often feels like a threat rather than a challenge, triggering our fight-or-flight response.

One key difference between eustress and distress lies in perception and control. When you feel you have what it takes to meet a challenge, stress can be invigorating and constructive. But when you feel powerless or unsupported, the same stressor can become distressing. This is why two people can experience the same event, such as public speaking, very differently: one may feel exhilarated, while the other feels paralyzed with fear. As odd as it may seem, I'd rather speak in front of a thousand people than a small group of ten!

Our reactions to stress, whether positive (eustress) or negative (distress), are deeply rooted in our biology and psychology. The human body is designed to respond to challenges through a system known as the stress response, which is governed by the brain and nervous system. This response is not inherently harmful. It evolved to help us survive. When we perceive a challenge, our brain signals the release of hormones like adrenaline and cortisol, which prepare the body to act. You've felt this—that surge before a big presentation, the heightened alertness when you narrowly avoid a car accident, the nervous energy before a first date. That's your stress response doing exactly what it evolved to do.

In the case of eustress, this response is brief and energizing. The heart rate increases slightly, focus sharpens, and the body feels alert and ready. This is the kind of stress that helps you meet a deadline, perform well in a competition, or rise to a new opportunity. Because the challenge is perceived as manageable and meaningful, the body returns to a state of balance once the task is complete. Eustress can even enhance memory, creativity, and problem-solving skills, reinforcing a sense of confidence and capability.

Distress, on the other hand, occurs when the stressor feels overwhelming or unrelenting. The same biological systems are activated, but instead of resolving quickly, the stress response lingers. Chronic exposure to distress keeps cortisol levels elevated, which can impair immune function, disrupt sleep, and contribute to anxiety and depression. Mentally, distress narrows our perspective, making it harder to think clearly or see solutions. Emotionally, it can lead to feelings of helplessness, frustration, or despair.

The key difference lies in how the brain interprets the situation. If a person believes they have the resources to cope, stress becomes motivating. If they feel powerless or unsupported, the same situation becomes harmful. This is why mindset, past experiences, and support systems play such a vital role in how we experience stress. Our thoughts, beliefs, and emotional resilience shape whether a challenge feels like a threat or an opportunity.

Understanding this mind-body connection empowers us to respond more intentionally to stress. By learning to recognize our internal signals such as racing thoughts, tension, and fatigue, we can pause, reflect, and choose healthier coping strategies. Practices like mindfulness, deep breathing, and seeking support can help shift our response from distress to eustress. When we treat our bodies and minds with compassion, we create space for healing and renewed strength.

Now that we understand what stress is and how it works, let's explore where it comes from. Because you can't manage what you don't understand.

The Sources of Stress

You can't always control what goes on outside. But you can always control what goes on inside. (Dyer)

Stress doesn't come from nowhere. It has roots: some deep, some shallow, some obvious, and some hidden. To manage stress effectively, we first need to understand where it's coming from.

Let's break stress into three major categories:

1. Major Life Events
2. Chronic Strains
3. Daily Hassles

Major Life Events

These are the big ones. These are the events that shake your world and demand a massive emotional response. Some are joyful, others painful but *all* are stressful. Can you recall any of these events happening in your own life? When was the last time that you experienced the death of a loved one? If you're a parent, recall the birth or adoption of your child. Have you ever been fired from a job? You might not have to think too hard to remember the visceral response that you had to these stressors. Unfortunately, life sometimes compounds these on us—often when enduring a divorce, moving to a new home, and even getting remarried all happen in a very short window.

Remember, too, that even positive changes can be stressful. A vacation, for example, might seem relaxing, but the planning, travel, and disruption to routine can still take a toll.

Change, even when it's good, requires
energy. And energy is a limited resource.

In a 1967 study, Holmes and Rahe developed The Social Readjustment Rating Scale (SRRS). The scale contained 43 life events (both positive and negative) and assigned a point value, or Life Change Unit (LCU), to each. The point values attempted to measure the impact of the event on physical health. As an example, "death of a spouse" ranked the highest on the scale at 100 LCUs. The more of these life events you've experienced in the past year, the higher your risk of stress-induced health issues in the next two years. You can take the interactive Holmes-Rahe Life Stress Inventory online at stress.org to calculate your own Life Change Units. A score of 150 or less suggests relatively low susceptibility, 150-300 indicates moderate risk (about 50% chance of stress-related health issues), and over 300 suggests high risk (about 80% chance). Understanding your number isn't about creating panic— it's about creating awareness. Keep in mind that the scale was developed in 1967, so the events are somewhat dated. If we were to update the scale, I'm certain that "Loss of Internet Connectivity for more than 4 hours" would rank well above many others!

Think back on the major events of your life. Remember how they seemed to impact everything else that was going on at the time. Maybe they were good: births, new jobs, marriage, exciting vacations. I'm sure, too, that your life story is sprinkled (or maybe flooded) with the not-so-good: deaths, divorce, incarceration. Looking back on these events allows us a different perspective, doesn't it? When we reflect, we realize that each of these things, good and bad, helped make us what we are today. When I present this topic in a workshop, I often ask participants to list some of the major events in their lives, both good and bad. Then, for each event, they are challenged to answer the question, "What's the learning?" In Viktor Frankl's book, *Man's Search for Meaning*, he concludes that when we can find new meaning from our suffering, we have overcome... and he was writing from the perspective of enduring a Nazi concentration camp! The book, *When Bad Things Happen to Good People*, is a great read when you seek meaning and perspective from life's chaos. Both authors implore us to go beyond the event, the suffering, the stress, and find a new reason to be happy... rediscover your uniqueness and your true self.

When nothing has to go right for us to be happy, and people do not have to behave for us to love them, our walk home becomes surprisingly simple. (Prather)

Chronic Strains

These are the slow burns. The ongoing pressures that wear you down over time. They don't always make headlines in your life, but they're always there gnawing at your energy, your confidence, and your peace of mind. These stressors are especially dangerous because they're persistent. You can't just "get over" them. They require long-term strategies and, often, outside support. Many times, they build on each other, compounding stress and anxiety. A good friend of mine, who has been through a lion's share of chronic stress, explained it this way. He asked, "Have you ever leaned back in your chair, and almost tipped back, but caught yourself just in time?" He said that he feels like that most days.

Let's look at several examples of chronic stress.

High-stress jobs

High-stress jobs expose individuals to prolonged and repeated psychological and physiological demands that exceed their coping resources. Unlike acute stress, which is short-term and often tied to specific events, chronic strain builds over time and can stem from constant pressure to meet deadlines, manage high workloads, or handle emotionally taxing environments which are common in professions like healthcare, law enforcement, education, and corporate leadership. This persistent exposure can lead to burnout, emotional exhaustion, and a range of health issues, including anxiety, depression, and heart problems. The unrelenting nature of these stressors makes recovery difficult, reinforcing a cycle of strain that can erode both personal well-being and professional performance. How does your job contribute to your "stress level"? Do you ever ask yourself, "Is it worth it"? That should tell you something!

Chronic illness (yours or a loved one's)

Living with a chronic illness or caring for a loved one who has one is a powerful example of chronic strain because it involves ongoing emotional, physical, and often financial stress that doesn't have a clear endpoint. The daily management of symptoms, medical appointments, and uncertainty about the future can create a persistent sense of vigilance and fatigue. For caregivers, the emotional toll of watching someone they love suffer, combined with the responsibilities of providing support, can lead to burnout and feelings of helplessness. This continuous exposure to stressors, without adequate time or space for recovery, can erode mental health, strain relationships, and diminish overall quality of life, making chronic illness a profound and enduring source of strain. Many of us have been or are caregivers right now. Resources are available for caregivers, so be sure to ask the patient's doctors, nurses, and social workers for support. As a caregiver, you're a critical part of your loved one's medical care team.

Financial insecurity

Financial instability is a powerful and pervasive chronic strain, with far-reaching consequences for mental, physical, and relational well-being. According to a 2025 Bankrate survey, 43% of U.S. adults report that money negatively impacts their mental health, with a majority citing difficulty paying for everyday expenses as a major source of stress. This kind of persistent financial pressure, whether from mounting debt, job insecurity, or the inability to build savings, creates a constant state of anxiety and uncertainty. For example, people with depression and debt problems are 4.2 times more likely to still have depression 18 months later than those without financial difficulties.

The physical toll is equally alarming. Chronic financial stress activates the body's stress response system, leading to elevated cortisol levels, inflammation, and long-term health risks. A 2024 study in *Brain, Behavior, and Immunity* found that individuals experiencing chronic stress showed distinct immune-neuroendocrine patterns associated with increased health risks, including heart disease, diabetes, and weakened immune function.

These effects are often compounded by unhealthy coping mechanisms like poor diet, substance use, and other self-destructive behaviors.

I can think of many real-life examples that illustrate how deeply financial instability can erode quality of life. Recently, a customer service representative on my team—we'll call her Maria—who was a single mother juggling multiple jobs, began avoiding bills due to overwhelming stress, leading to missed payments and worsening debt. Every time her personal cell phone rang, she dreaded answering, certain that it was a debt collector. Another former colleague, Alex, a young professional, turned to impulsive "doom spending" to cope with anxiety over student loans, only to spiral further into financial insecurity. He said that he was always "rich" on payday.

Relationships also suffer under chronic financial strain. Disagreements about money are a leading cause of conflict in couples, and women who frequently argue about money in marriage are nearly three times more likely to divorce. Financial infidelity, such as hiding purchases or debts is also common, eroding trust and intimacy.

Financial instability is not just an economic issue, it is a chronic, multifaceted strain that affects every layer of a person's life. Addressing it requires both systemic solutions and personal strategies, including financial education, mental health support, and access to resources that promote long-term stability.

Food insecurity

Food insecurity is a profound example of chronic strain, as it imposes ongoing psychological, emotional, and physical stress on individuals and families who lack consistent access to enough nutritious food. In 2023, 13.5% of U.S. households, about 18 million, experienced food insecurity, with 6.8 million facing very low food security, meaning their eating patterns were disrupted due to lack of resources.

This persistent uncertainty about where the next meal will come from creates a constant state of anxiety and vigilance, which can erode mental health over time. A comprehensive meta-analysis found that food insecurity increases the odds of psychological distress by 329%, with strong links to depression, anxiety, sleep problems, and lower life satisfaction.

The impact begins early: children in food-insecure households often experience toxic stress, which can impair brain development, emotional regulation, and academic performance. Adults, meanwhile, may suffer from cognitive fatigue, irritability, and shame, which can lead to social withdrawal and difficulty maintaining employment or relationships.

These effects are not just emotional: food insecurity is also associated with higher rates of chronic illnesses such as diabetes, hypertension, and obesity, as individuals often resort to cheaper, less nutritious food options when resources are scarce. Eating a healthy diet can be expensive!

We all know of , or maybe have been, the single parent working multiple jobs who may skip meals to ensure their children eat. A college student might rely on food pantries and still go to bed hungry, affecting their concentration and academic success. These are not isolated incidents but part of a broader systemic issue that affects nearly 47.4 million people in the U.S. And, as I write this chapter in the fall of 2025, efforts are underway to make it even more difficult to access food as federal cuts to the SNAP (Supplemental Nutritional Assistance Program) are being enacted.

Food insecurity is not just about hunger, it's about the chronic, compounding stress of living without a basic human need. Addressing it requires not only food assistance but also policies that tackle the root causes, such as poverty, housing instability, and healthcare access.

Lack of a support system

Lack of a support system is a powerful example of chronic strain because it deprives individuals of the emotional, social, and practical resources needed to cope with life's ongoing challenges. When people face stressors such as illness, job loss, parenting demands, or grief without the buffer of supportive relationships, the burden becomes heavier and more persistent. Research shows that social isolation and loneliness are linked to increased levels of cortisol, the stress hormone, and are associated with higher risks of depression, anxiety, and even premature death. For example, individuals without strong social ties are 29% more likely to develop coronary heart disease and 32% more likely to experience a stroke (Valtorta et al., 2016). The absence of a support system can also lead to decision fatigue, emotional exhaustion, and a sense of helplessness, as there is no one to share responsibilities, offer encouragement, or provide a different perspective. Over time, this unrelenting emotional load can erode resilience and make even manageable stressors feel overwhelming, reinforcing a cycle of chronic strain.

Look at some real-life examples that illustrate how the lack of a support system can become a source of chronic strain:

Elderly individuals living alone often face ongoing emotional and physical challenges without anyone to assist them. For instance, an older adult recovering from surgery may struggle with mobility, medication management, and loneliness, which can lead to delayed healing and depression. Without family or community support, even simple tasks become overwhelming, creating a constant state of stress.

Single parents without extended family or community support frequently experience chronic strain. A mother working two jobs to support her children may have no one to help with childcare or school responsibilities. The constant juggling of responsibilities without relief can lead to anxiety and burnout.

Young adults aging out of foster care often lack a stable support network. Without consistent guidance, they may struggle with employment and emotional regulation. This absence of support increases their risk of substance use and mental health challenges.

Immigrants or refugees who are separated from their families and communities may face language barriers, cultural isolation, and discrimination. Without a support system, they often carry the full weight of adapting to a new environment alone, which can lead to chronic stress and feelings of alienation.

Professionals in high-stress careers, such as healthcare workers or first responders, may not have the emotional support they need to process trauma or exhaustion. Without peers or loved ones to confide in, they may internalize stress, leading to compassion-fatigue and burnout.

These examples show that the absence of a support system doesn't just make life harder, it compounds stress over time, turning everyday challenges into chronic emotional burdens.

For those who work in any field of human services, you realize that most, if not all, of your clients struggle with chronic stressors. Have you ever noticed, too, that some people just seem to be magnets for unfortunate events in life? You know who I'm talking about. It's a friend or relative who just cannot seem to ever "get it together". They seem to be on a rat wheel and can never get off. Maybe it's you.

Do you seem to always be trying to deal with a never-ending barrage of misfortune? Does the lack of a support system cause an avalanche of events that create additional stress, anxiety, and hopelessness? Does your lack of coping skills negatively impact your ability to overcome struggle and strife?

Consider this hypothetical, but all-too-common scenario:

> *Bill is divorced but has his kids this week. He didn't plan all that well for them... probably forgetting again that it was his turn. He wanted to get a little overtime to try to pay some bills. Then, he gets a call from school that his daughter has a fever. His boss gives him hell about leaving, because he has no leave time available, but he has no one else to get her. On his way, he has a flat tire. He doesn't have roadside assistance. Can't afford it. He changes the tire to the very bald spare and hopes it will last until he can get a new one... with what money, he could not tell you. He tried to call the school to let them know that he was on his way, but he didn't pay his cell phone bill again this month. This is what chronic strain looks like—not one catastrophic event, but an unrelenting series of setbacks that compound on each other until even the smallest task feels insurmountable.*

Daily Hassles

We've all heard the expression, "Death by a thousand cuts". What literally used to be a brutal method of execution serves as a strong metaphor for a slow, yet persistent, accumulation of stress caused by seemingly innocuous, minor setbacks. These are the little things. The annoyances, interruptions, and irritations that pile up throughout the day.

Individually, they're manageable. But when they stack up, especially on top of major life events or chronic strains, they can push you over the edge. We all handle traffic, spilled coffee, and mudpuddles just fine. But when compounded, these quickly wear us down.

Interestingly, too, some of these "hassles" can also be "uplifts." Your kids might drive you crazy one minute and melt your heart the next. I love when the mom says, "Oh, my baby got an A on her test in math!" and then, 30 minutes later, the mom screams at the girl's dad, "Do you know what *your* daughter just said?" A busy day at work might be exhausting but also fulfilling. It's all about perspective.

A 1982 study from DeLongis, Folkman, and Lazarus, *The Impact of Daily Stress on Health and Mood*, explored this topic in "The Hassles and Uplifts Scale". The questionnaire contains a topic or event that can either be considered to be an uplift or a hassle, or both. Participants are asked to assess each item to what degree the prompt was a hassle or an uplift for the day. (It is recommended to complete the scale immediately before bed, considering the items from the day.)

For example, a prompt could ask, how much of a hassle or uplift today were your children? Respondents circle the degree to which their children were hassles and/or uplifts. 0 = none; 1 =

somewhat; 2 = quite a bit; 3 = a great deal. Visually, the scale might appear like so:

Hassles		Uplifts
0 1 2 3	Your Children	0 1 2 3
0 1 2 3	The Weather	0 1 2 3
0 1 2 3	Yardwork	0 1 2 3

The scale is designed for awareness. Some hassles occur more frequently than others while some uplifts can be counted on for joy in your life!

Reflection Prompt

Take five minutes and list:

- Three major life events you've experienced in the past year

- Two chronic strains you're currently facing

- Five daily hassles that regularly frustrate you

- Five uplifts that you can count on for happiness

Now circle the ones you can control. Put a star next to the ones you can't. This exercise isn't about fixing everything, it's about clarity. And clarity is power.

Recognizing the Symptoms

The body whispers before it screams.
(Reynolds)

In this chapter, we're going to identify symptoms of stress by taking the same approach you would when visiting a doctor. You don't walk in and say, "I think my white blood cell count is low and I may have a 2.5 cm lesion on C5." You say, "My back hurts, and I've had a headache for six months." In other words, you start with what and how you feel.

This chapter is about tuning in, learning to listen to the signals your body and mind are sending. Because emotional exhaustion doesn't happen overnight. It builds slowly and quietly. Stress also doesn't always announce itself with sirens and flashing lights. And if you're not paying attention, it can take hold before you even realize it's there. The sooner you recognize the signs, the sooner you can respond with intention.

One of the first signs is persistent fatigue, even after a full night's sleep. This isn't just physical tiredness, it's a deep, soul-level weariness that makes even simple tasks feel overwhelming. People may find themselves waking up already dreading the day, lacking the energy or motivation to engage in activities they once enjoyed. This fatigue is often accompanied by a sense of detachment or numbness, where emotions feel blunted or distant.

Another early indicator is increased irritability or emotional sensitivity. Small inconveniences may trigger outsized reactions, or individuals may find themselves crying more easily or feeling unusually anxious. This emotional volatility is often a sign that the nervous system is under strain. People may also begin to withdraw from social interactions, not because they don't care, but because they simply don't have the emotional bandwidth to engage.

Cognitive symptoms are also common. Difficulty concentrating, forgetfulness, and a sense of mental fog can make it hard to stay focused or make decisions. Tasks that once felt routine may now seem insurmountable. This mental fatigue can lead to a drop in performance at work or school, which in turn can increase feelings of inadequacy or guilt, further deepening the emotional exhaustion.

Finally, emotional exhaustion often manifests in physical symptoms such as headaches, muscle tension, digestive issues, or changes in appetite and sleep patterns. These physical signs are the body's way of signaling that something is out of balance. When these symptoms are ignored or minimized, they can evolve into more serious health concerns. Recognizing these early signs is not a sign of weakness, it's an act of self-awareness and self-compassion. If you or someone you know is experiencing these symptoms, it's important to seek support and begin the journey toward restoration and resilience.

I would like to place four caveats on any interpretation of these symptoms:

1. They exist on a continuum.
2. You must eliminate the physical aspects first.
3. Chronicity and constellation are important.
4. Isolated symptoms are probably insignificant.

A Symptom Continuum

Continuum is one of those quirky words with double *u*s like vacuum and it's one whose definition I will never forget, thanks to an early college psychology class. I can still hear my beloved professor (who later became my therapist) explaining, "A continuum is a graphic, linear representation of an abstract idea or concept that can't be easily compartmentalized or segmented." In other words, it's a line we use to represent things that don't fit neatly into boxes. Helpful? Sort of.

In our workshops, I will sometimes ask participants to form an imaginary line in the front of the room. Chocolate lovers go to my far right and chocolate haters to my far left... and those who remain can scatter somewhere in between. Where you place yourself on this "chocolate continuum" is based on your preference for chocolate. There's no precise scale. No one says, "I like chocolate at a level 78." And if I offered my wife a piece of dark chocolate with a glass of merlot, she'd probably shift a little further to the right. That's the nature of a continuum: placement is fluid.

The same is true for the thirteen major symptoms of stress we'll explore in this chapter. Each one exists along a continuum of severity. This is a crucial lens through which to view them. Symptoms of stress can't easily be measured. Their severity and impact vary in individuals and certainly among different people. We all tolerate stress differently and our symptoms present themselves to varying degrees.

Eliminate the physical aspects first

I once advised a student who began experiencing sudden panic attacks: shortness of breath, heavy sweating, and a sense of overwhelming fear. These episodes struck at unpredictable times: before or after tests, during sports games, or even in the middle of class. When we reached out to his parents, they assured us his physical health was fine. But let's be honest—a standard school sports physical (the classic "turn and cough") isn't exactly a comprehensive medical evaluation. With some gentle persistence, the student was eventually taken for a full medical workup. His diagnosis? Stress-induced asthma. A daily maintenance medication and a rescue inhaler resolved what had been mistaken for panic attacks.

The takeaway here comes courtesy of Occam's razor: sometimes the simplest explanation is the right one. Before jumping to conclusions, make sure your nausea and vomiting aren't just the result of last night's bad sushi.

Chronicity and Constellation

Life naturally comes with highs and lows. We understand this, and most of the time, we know how to navigate it. It can be exhausting, yes, but it's also what makes life dynamic and meaningful.

When we talk about stress symptoms, it's important to distinguish between what's acute and what's chronic. A migraine every six months is very different from one or two a week. As always, start by ruling out physical causes and don't skip the medical checkup. Then ask yourself, "How persistent are these symptoms? How often do they show up?"

Another helpful concept is constellation. This is when symptoms cluster around a specific event, memory, or situation. Can you trace certain reactions to particular triggers? Do you break out in hives when your in-laws come to dinner? Does your heart race before staff meetings? What, or who, "pushes your buttons"? While correlation doesn't always mean causation, it's still worth paying attention to. If your symptoms tend to "constellate" around certain experiences, your body might be trying to tell you something important.

Isolated symptoms

Finally, in this age where technology is always at our fingertips, it's easy to fall into the trap of diagnosing every symptom with a quick internet search. But let's be honest, if your medical degree is from Google University (go Dodo Birds!), it might be time to take a step back. Constantly searching for the root cause of every ache, mood swing, or forgotten birthday will only drive you up the wall. Sometimes you'll snap at your dog, feel sad after a loss, or forget to text a friend back. That's not a crisis; it's called being human. So, give yourself the same grace you so freely offer others. That's not just self-care; it's the foundation of a more peaceful, fulfilling life.

The 13 Symptoms

Overactivity

In adults, we might call it manic, in kids, hyper, though the ideas here apply across all ages. Younger people are just as stressed as we are. Either way, it looks like someone hit fast-forward on your life. You're constantly "on," buzzing with energy, unable to sit still. You're overcommitted, running on adrenaline, and bouncing from one task to the next like a sprayed cockroach. You touch everything, talk nonstop, fidget, pace, and multitask yourself into exhaustion.

We've all heard of the person who has a rough week at work and then spends the entire weekend deep cleaning the house, reorganizing the garage, and alphabetizing the spice rack. Or the friend who, after a stressful breakup, signs up for three new fitness classes and starts a side hustle all in the same week.

Many times, overactivity can be a substitute for a more appropriately paced life. Individuals under stress might attempt to prove themselves with volunteering, feeling like they have to engage in every decision being made at work, or reading ten books in a weekend.

Overactivity can feel productive on the surface, but it's often a way to try to outrun grief and anxiety. It's motion without rest, effort without pause. And while it may look impressive, it's never sustainable in the long run.

Underactivity

One of the most overlooked symptoms of stress and emotional exhaustion is underactivity. Unlike the frantic energy of overactivity, this shows up as a slow fade. You feel drained, sluggish, and unmotivated. Even simple tasks, like getting out of bed, answering a text, or making a meal can feel overwhelming. You begin to withdraw from activities you once enjoyed. Conversations become shorter or stop altogether. Your focus drifts, your concentration slips, and your world starts to shrink.

This isn't laziness. It's your body and mind signaling that they're overwhelmed. Think of the friend who used to be the life of the group chat but now leaves messages unread for days. Or the coworker who once thrived on collaboration but now keeps their camera off and voice muted in every meeting. Or maybe it's you. Do you find yourself canceling plans, skipping workouts, or zoning out in front of the TV for hours without really watching anything. How many cat videos will it take?

You might find yourself "underachieving" in your normal routines. When your lawn was a source of great pride, now you mow on a routine schedule, but trim hedges just on occasion. When you would ensure that you changed the oil in the car every 3,000 miles, you shrug it off at 5,000. You tell yourself that it will wait. You become adept at lame excuses for "not" doing and "not" showing up. It is clearly unlike you.

Underactivity can be a non-clinical precursor to depression, and it deserves just as much attention as more visible signs of stress. Recognizing it early gives you the chance to respond with care, rather than criticism.

Tension-Reducing Behaviors

These are ways we try, often unconsciously, to cope with stress, especially when it builds up without a healthy outlet. These behaviors can range from mildly unhelpful to downright risky. Perhaps you find yourself overeating, binge-watching shows for hours, scrolling endlessly through social media, or reaching for alcohol or other substances more often than usual. Some people become overly talkative, what we sometimes call "motor-mouthing", to release nervous energy. Others might seek out adrenaline through reckless activities like speeding, impulsive and compulsive spending, or thrill-seeking adventures. (Motorbiking without a helmet, anyone?)

This is also where psychological defense mechanisms come into play. Displacement, for example, is when you redirect your stress or frustration onto something or someone less threatening. You have a terrible day at work, come home, and yell at your spouse or kick at the dog. On the flip side, there's sublimation, a more constructive defense mechanism. This is when you channel stress into something positive, like going for a run, hitting the gym, painting, or throwing yourself into a creative project. It's still a release, but one that builds you up rather than breaks you down.

The key is to recognize these behaviors for what they are: signals. They're not inherently good or bad, but they do tell you something important about how you're managing your stress and whether it's time to pause and recalibrate.

Psychosomatic Symptoms

This is your body's way of waving a red flag when your mind is under strain. These are real, physical symptoms that are either triggered or worsened by emotional stress. Common examples include headaches, stomachaches, muscle tension, fatigue, and sleep disturbances. But the list doesn't stop there. Stress can also contribute to blurred vision, hives, high blood pressure, rapid heartbeat (tachycardia), and even gastrointestinal issues like irritable bowel syndrome (IBS) or acid reflux.

In some cases, chronic stress may weaken the immune system, making you more susceptible to colds or infections. It can also exacerbate existing conditions like eczema, fibromyalgia, or heart disease. And yes, ulcers, once thought to be caused solely by stress, can still be aggravated by it, even if the root cause is bacterial.

Sometimes, these symptoms are subtle. Other times, they're loud and disruptive. Either way, they're not "just in your head." They're your body's way of saying, *"Something's not right."* That's why it's essential to listen. If you experience sudden or persistent physical symptoms, especially chest pain, shortness of breath, or dizziness, don't self-diagnose. <u>Seek medical advice immediately.</u> Stress may be the culprit, but it's always best to rule out other serious conditions first.

Emotional Variability

One of the more exhausting symptoms of stress and emotional overload is emotional variability. It's that roller-coaster feeling of swinging from laughter to tears, from calm to frustration, often with no clear trigger. One moment you're energized and optimistic, the next you're overwhelmed and irritable. These emotional shifts can be rapid, intense, and confusing not just for you, but for those around you.

Imagine how those around you feel when they can no longer anticipate or predict your reactions to everyday events. It is extremely telling to those around you when you don't take things seriously as you once did or if you overreact to something that is really nothing. If the people around you begin to mention this, pay attention!

Think back to a time when you cried deeply whether from sadness or joy. Chances are, you felt physically drained afterward. That's because strong emotions take a toll on your body as well as your mind. Now imagine experiencing those highs and lows repeatedly throughout the day. It's no wonder emotional variability often leads to fatigue, brain fog, and a sense of being emotionally "on edge."

You might find yourself snapping at a loved one, tearing up during a commercial, or laughing uncontrollably at something only mildly funny. These aren't signs of weakness. They're signs that your emotional system is working overtime. And while occasional mood swings are normal, persistent emotional volatility may be a signal that your stress levels are pushing past your capacity to cope.

Negative Thoughts and Feelings

Negativity often creeps in when stress and emotional exhaustion take hold. You may start to feel hopeless, irritable, or overwhelmed. It can feel like nothing will ever get better, and that sense of despair can turn inward, fueling self-doubt and low self-esteem. Or it can turn outward, making you more impatient, judgmental, or resentful toward others. You might catch yourself thinking, *"What's the point?"* or *"Why bother?"* These thoughts erode your motivation and sense of worth.

This isn't just about having a bad day. It's a deeper, more persistent negativity that colors how you see yourself and the world. It's different from the "crabby uncle" we all know: the one who's been perpetually grumpy since 1959 and would complain about winning the lottery because the check came late. The kind of negativity that we are talking about is often new, uncharacteristic, and tied to emotional depletion.

When you don't have the emotional fortitude to honestly celebrate your grandchild's score at a soccer game or your wife's promotion, you need to explore the reasons why. Are you jealous of the success of others? Did you have similar experiences only to have them discounted?

You might find yourself withdrawing from people, assuming the worst in situations, or feeling like you're failing even when you're doing your best. These thoughts can be subtle or loud, but either way, they're draining. Recognizing them is the first step toward challenging them and replacing them with something more compassionate and grounded.

Anxiety

Anxiety often shows up as a racing mind that just won't quit. You worry constantly about things that have happened, things that might happen, and even things that probably never will. It can feel like there's a low-level alarm always going off in the background, warning you that something bad is just around the corner. One of the most important aspects of anxiety is its severity. Occasional worry is normal, but when it becomes excessive, irrational, or persistent, it can interfere with daily life. My wife showed me a comic recently of a frazzled woman holding a sign that read, "98% of the things I worried about never happened. See, worrying works!"

You might experience "worrying about worrying" which is a secondary disturbance where the anxiety itself becomes the source of more anxiety. For example, you're anxious about a job interview tomorrow, but now you're also anxious that you won't sleep well tonight… which makes it even harder to sleep. This kind of mental spiral is exhausting.

We've all heard of "paralysis by analysis" those times when you overthink even simple decisions, like what to wear, what to say in an email, or whether to send a text. You might rehearse conversations in your head, second-guess your choices, or avoid making decisions altogether. Other signs include restlessness, muscle tension, difficulty concentrating, and a constant sense of being "on edge."

Anxiety can be sneaky. It doesn't always look like panic. It can look like perfectionism, procrastination, irritability, or even physical symptoms like stomachaches or headaches. The key is to notice the patterns and recognize when your mind is working overtime in ways that aren't serving you.

Sleep Issues

Suffering from sleep issues is one of the most common and most disruptive signs of stress and emotional exhaustion. You might struggle to fall asleep, wake up frequently during the night, or rise in the morning feeling just as tired as when you went to bed. Your rest isn't restful. For some, sleep issues show up as insomnia, too little sleep. For others, it's hypersomnia, sleeping too much, yet still feeling drained.

Stress can also affect the quality of your sleep. You might experience vivid dreams or nightmares, or find that you're not reaching deep, restorative REM sleep, which is essential for emotional processing and memory consolidation. Some people report not dreaming at all, which can be a sign of disrupted sleep cycles. Others may experience sleepwalking, sleep talking, or even teeth grinding (bruxism), all physical signs that your body is carrying stress into the night.

You might also notice behavioral changes: falling asleep on the couch during the day, relying on caffeine or those energy drinks to stay alert, or feeling mentally foggy despite getting "enough" hours of sleep. These are all signs that your sleep is being affected not just by your schedule, but by your stress levels. How many of you worry about not sleeping enough because you go to bed and a thousand things keep racing in your mind? I was once given that proverbial sage advice to "count sheep". Well, I counted them alright... and then named them, and then sheared them, and then arranged them by size. I realized that it wasn't working when I finally had to get up and research at what temperature mutton is cooked!

Speech Issues

Having speech issues can be also a subtle but telling sign of stress and emotional fatigue. You might find yourself stumbling over words, losing your train of thought mid-sentence, or struggling to express yourself clearly. When I'm overly tired or stressed, I tend to stutter. For me it is a personal reminder that my brain and body are out of sync. Others may repeat themselves, as if trying to reassure themselves or regain control. I know someone who, when asked, "How are you?" often replies, "Oh, pretty good... pretty good." It's as if he's trying to convince himself of the answer.

You might also notice word-finding difficulties, where common words suddenly feel just out of reach, or parapraxes, better known as Freudian slips, where your words accidentally reveal what's really on your mind. For example, saying "I'm stressed" instead of "I'm blessed" in a conversation meant to sound upbeat.

Other signs include speaking more quickly or more slowly than usual, trailing off mid-thought, or using filler words excessively ("um," "like," "you know") as your brain tries to catch up. In high-stress moments, some people even go completely quiet, not out of rudeness, but because forming coherent thoughts feels too overwhelming.

These speech disruptions aren't signs of incompetence. They're signs that your cognitive load is maxed out. Your mind is multitasking under pressure, and your words are simply showing the strain.

Resistance or Submission

These are two common, yet opposite, responses to stress and both can signal that your emotional reserves are running low. On one end of the continuum, you might find yourself pushing back against everything. Even simple, routine requests feel like personal attacks. Your boss asks, "Can you bring me the Smith files?" and you explode: "GET OFF MY BACK! WHY CAN'T SUSIE BRING THEM TO YOU?" The reaction is disproportionate, but it comes from a place of emotional overload.

On the other end, you might give in to everyone. You stop asserting your needs, your boundaries dissolve, and you say "yes" to everything even when it's too much. You might agree to take on extra work, cancel personal plans, or avoid conflict at all costs, just to keep the peace. To a greater extent, you might give in to requests or situations you're uncomfortable with, compromising your own boundaries and well-being. Over time, this kind of submission can lead to resentment, burnout, and a loss of self-confidence.

These behaviors often show up in subtle ways too. You might roll your eyes at a harmless suggestion, ghost a group chat because you don't have the energy to engage, or agree to something and immediately regret it. It is quite easy to be taken advantage of when you're going through this. Whether you're resisting or submitting, the common thread is that your stress is dictating your behavior, not your values or intentions. Passive aggressive tendencies emerge from otherwise direct people.

Depression

It is not always evident that you're experiencing depression. But by focusing on the subtle, early signs of depression you can identify and more easily manage the symptoms before they become overwhelming. Caught early, depression can be very treatable.

Although most of us have days when we are not quite our cheerful selves, depression is much more pervasive. You may feel emotionally numb, persistently sad, or as if you're carrying an invisible weight that never lifts. It can manifest as a deep sense of hopelessness, guilt, or worthlessness, even when there's no clear reason. You might lose interest in activities that once brought you joy like hobbies, socializing, or even simple daily routines. The mere idea of doing these things seems too much to handle.

People experiencing depression easily become overwhelmed by what others would consider minor hassles. Losing your car keys might evoke despair rather than mild annoyance. Usual routines such as paying bills, washing the car, and buying groceries all seem insurmountable. We've all heard the phrase 'too difficult to even get out of bed.' When you're depressed, that's not an exaggeration. Depression grabs you by the throat and doesn't let go easily. Instead of getting back up when life knocks you down, staying on the ground feels easier.

Unfortunately, underlying depression can also appear as other symptoms: symptoms of depression appear in some people as changes in appetite or sleep patterns, such as sleeping too much or too little, or eating significantly more or less than usual. Others may struggle with concentration, decision-making, or feel unusually fatigued despite resting.

You might find yourself with irrational thoughts that make you question yourself. You think, "I don't care", "It will probably turn out badly", "So what?". In turn, you begin to pull back and isolate yourself. While alone time is a very necessary part of a healthy lifestyle, individuals suffering from depression may purposefully avoid others in a desire to "separate". Like a wounded animal, you may retreat to your cave and fight the urge to leave it.

It's important to understand that these symptoms can occur even if a clinical diagnosis hasn't been made. Be mindful of these signs in yourself and **others. If you or someone you know is showing signs of depression, seek professional help. Early support can make a significant difference.**

Unconsciousness

In extreme cases of stress or emotional overload, your body and mind may begin to shut down as a form of self-protection. This can manifest in several ways: you might faint, dissociate, or feel completely disconnected from your surroundings. You may even repress certain emotions, memories, or experiences without realizing it.

One common phenomenon is "losing time". Have you ever driven for 10 or 15 minutes and suddenly realized you don't remember the journey? That's called *highway hypnosis*, and it's more common than you might think. Similarly, you might find yourself staring into space, unaware of how much time has passed. My wife often catches me doing this outside. I call it my "thinking time." She has another, not so positive word for it.

Just the feeling of "passing out" is indicative of stress. Suddenly feeling dizzy or lightheaded, feeling like the floor is moving beneath your feet, and becoming aware of the possibility of your fainting, each can be a sign that the stress in your daily life is becoming unmanageable. Again, be sure to rule out physical possibilities; if you have diabetes, check your blood sugar according to your physician's instructions. As someone with diabetes, I generally can tell when my glucose levels are out-of-whack... and I know the difference between it being a feeling of stress or not enough food.

Other examples include walking into a room and forgetting why you went there or rereading the same paragraph repeatedly without absorbing the words. These are all subtle signs that your mind is trying to disconnect in order to cope.

Changes in Habits and Behaviors

Stress and emotional exhaustion often show up in shifts to our established patterns—changes that might seem unrelated at first but often share a common thread: they're attempts to cope, escape, or numb difficult emotions.

Eating Habits/Substance Use

Eating habits may shift. You might overeat, undereat, or find yourself "stress eating" as a form of comfort. Someone who might otherwise be a very light, social drinker of alcohol may find that they drink more often and much more than they used to. Individuals who are anxious about their weight may try sequential fad diets yet see no lasting benefits from any.

Compulsive Behaviors

Compulsive behaviors can also emerge, such as excessive gambling, shopping, or consuming pornography. These behaviors often serve as temporary distractions from deeper emotional pain.

I know several adults who constantly feel the need to shop and they will tell you that it "makes them happy". But when you take a closer look and talk to them about it, they will indicate that it is not *what* they bought, but the shopping itself that they find comforting. And they will admit that they have to continue to shop in order to feel good.

You might also develop phobias or obsessive thoughts that seem irrational but feel impossible to control. In more intimate areas of life, stress can lead to sexual dysfunction or a loss of desire. In extreme cases, people may even rationalize harmful decisions such as engaging in an extramarital affair to escape or feel something different.

Other signs include compulsive scrolling on social media, binge-watching shows to avoid thinking or constantly needing to stay busy to avoid being alone with your thoughts. These coping mechanisms may seem harmless at first, but over time, they can erode your well-being and relationships.

Normal Doesn't Mean Healthy

Here's the kicker: many of these symptoms are common. You might even think they're "just part of life." But just because something is common doesn't mean it's normal or healthy.

If you're experiencing several of these symptoms regularly, it's time to pause and reflect. Not to judge yourself. Not to panic. But to acknowledge that your system is overloaded and needs care.

The Power of Awareness

Awareness is the first step toward healing. When you can name what you're feeling, you can begin to manage it. You can ask for help. You can make changes. You can take your power back.

Remember our continuum? **On one end** of the continuum, it might just be a symptom of normal stress... but **on the other end**, it could be a significant mental health issue that requires professional guidance.

Reflection Prompt

Take a moment to check in on yourself:

- Which of the 13 symptoms have you experienced in the past week? month?

- Which ones show up most often?

- Which ones are you most likely to ignore?

Write them down. Talk about them with someone you trust. Or just sit with them for a while. You won't fix everything today. But you would do well to start noticing.

Reframing & Finding Your Main Thing

Grant me the serenity to accept the things I cannot change, courage to change the things I can, and wisdom to know the difference. (Niebuhr)

I vividly remember the day that my mother's doctor, who happened to also be mine, called me on my cell phone. "Eric, your mother has cancer." That diagnosis was not necessarily a surprise. The fact that she had smoked what we calculated to be over a quarter million cigarettes in her life cushioned the lung cancer diagnosis. We all expected it. At the time, my mother was living with me and my family. I had recently started a new job, and my marriage was equally young. She did not have insurance, so we had to navigate the Medicaid rat maze just to cover her medicine. The schedule of chemo and radiation drained what little PTO that I had, so we had to resort first to Medicaid transport, and finally to seeking a facility. I will not continue this story here for it would serve no purpose. Just understand that we all face cumulative stressors. We're forced to juggle work crises, sick parents, financial stress, and more—where everything feels equally urgent and important, and you feel like you simply cannot do enough. That paralysis, when you don't know where to focus, is crippling. So how do you find your footing when everything is falling apart at once?

Stress is so much more than our reaction to what happens to us, it's also about how we interpret and prioritize what happens to us. Two people can experience the same event and walk away with completely different reactions. Why? Because our perception shapes our reality.

This chapter is about learning how to reframe how you see your stressors and shift your mindset. It is about learning how to stop allowing stress to control your narrative and start writing a new one. It is about finding your "Main Thing" and allowing it to become your north star. It is about what truly matters the most.

In this chapter, we'll explore a practical framework for sorting your stressors and a values-based approach to finding your focus.

The Four Quadrants of Control

Various individuals and groups use a "4-quadrant" tool in their work. Covey popularized it in an "important/not-important, urgent/non-urgent" paradigm as it relates to time management. We are adapting it for stress management with an "important/not important", "can control/cannot control" schema.

When you can sort your stressors, you can respond more strategically. The 4-quadrant tool that we will discuss will ask you to place your stressors into one of the following quadrants:

Quadrant 1. Important – Can Control

These are your sweet spots. These are the areas where your energy is best spent and where you can effectuate change and growth. This includes things like your health habits (diet, exercise, and sleep), how you communicate with loved ones, your financial choices within your income, your time management and boundaries, and your response to difficult situations. Focus here. This is where real change happens.

My wife is an avid runner with over 25 marathons to her credit. Running isn't just what she does; it's who she is. Her running is very important to her psyche. When she is heavily into a training cycle, it is typical for her to be logging 50 to 60 miles per week. A few years ago, she was on an early morning run when a distracted driver hit her as she crossed the road at an intersection. He ran over her foot, crushing those bones. The impact knocked her to the ground, shattering an elbow, and the hand that she instinctively threw up to protect herself was also badly damaged. Fast forward to the fifth day in the hospital when an orthopedic surgeon came into her room to discuss her surgical options. Her mind had been going through all sorts of inner dialogue for days, but before he even got started, she asked: "Okay, so if you must amputate my foot, how fast can you put one of those blades on it? I am in the middle of a training cycle for a marathon that I *will* be running!" We will talk more about resilience later but was this an important event in our lives? Yes. Could my wife control her outlook on the event? Yes!

Quadrant 2. Important – Can't Control

These are the hardest. Things that matter deeply but are out of your hands such as a loved one's illness or choices; a company-wide layoff; natural disasters; someone else's addiction or behavior; and even the economy or politics. Here, your job is to accept and adapt. Not to give up, but to stop fighting what you can't fix.

We live in an area that has endured four, once-in-500-year floods in the past 20 years. Apparently, Mother Nature cannot do simple division. The first flood was the result of a major hurricane that delivered over 24" of rain in about as many hours. We saw rescue motorboats traveling down our street. We also saw refrigerators floating down it as well. We all knew what was coming but also realized that we were helpless in stopping it. So, what did our neighborhood do? We brought extra generators to each other. Our neighbor, the pharmacist, was chauffeured in a canoe to deliver medicines. A farmer with a very tall tractor and trailer took people a few miles away to a grocery store that managed to stay open for food and supplies. While we couldn't control the flood, we certainly did control our responses. That's the essence of Quadrant 2: accepting what you cannot change while choosing how you'll adapt.

Quadrant 3. Not Important – Can Control

These are the distractions. These are the things that feel urgent but aren't truly meaningful. These things steal your energy from what truly matters. Say no to these or delegate them or just ignore them! Think about how social media arguments, the weather or traffic, or other people's opinions of you can quickly become stressful if allowed to. Let them go. Reclaim your time and energy.

When I was Headmaster at a private school, one exasperated parent came to my office apologizing for being late, again. She explained that she argues every morning with her 8-year-old daughter over what to wear. We had no dress code for lower school students, and what the girl chose would have been perfectly fine. But this mother couldn't bear the thought of other mothers judging her for mismatched outfits. Daily battles over something that truly didn't matter: a perfect example of Quadrant 3.

Quadrant 4. Not Important – Can't Control

These things are pure noise. They don't matter and can't be changed. These include things such as celebrity gossip, political drama that you cannot influence, what someone said five years ago, and anything in the past! Release them. They're not worth your peace.

52

When we seriously consider this quadrant, we realize that a great deal of stress and anxiety originates from things we place here, concerns that neither matter deeply nor respond to our efforts. Learning to recognize and release Quadrant 4 stressors is a skill we'll develop throughout this book.

I once worked with someone who spent hours each week rehashing a workplace conflict from three years prior, long after the other person had moved to a different company. The situation was over, unchangeable, and frankly no longer relevant to anyone's current work. Yet the mental energy spent reliving it was exhausting. That's Quadrant 4: holding onto things that don't matter and can't be changed.

Now that you understand the four quadrants, let's explore how to actually use them. That's where reframing comes in.

The Practice of Reframing

Reframing is the skill of stepping back and seeing your stressors through a different lens. It's not about denying the pressure; it's about changing your relationship to it. You don't have to solve everything in the moment, but if you shift your perspective from helplessness to possibility, from isolation to support, you become in control.

Reframing doesn't mean pretending everything is fine. It means choosing a lens that empowers you instead of paralyzing you. Let's walk through a typical scenario with some examples:

Maria is a working parent navigating a typical weekday. She wakes up early to get her kids ready for school, rushes through traffic to make it to a morning meeting, and juggles emails while worrying about her aging father's health. Her phone buzzes constantly—some messages are urgent, others trivial. She's behind on a work deadline, her daughter forgot her lunch, and she just saw a news alert about rising interest rates. By mid-afternoon, she's exhausted, overwhelmed, and unsure what to focus on first.

So, for Maria, she might list the following stressors on a given day:

- A coworker's negative attitude in the break room

- Checking social media notifications during work hours

- Economic uncertainty and rising interest rates affecting her mortgage

- Finishing the work deadline that affects her performance review

- Following up with her daughter's teacher about missing assignments

- Her father's declining health and upcoming medical tests

- Responding to a group text about weekend plans

- Traffic delays due to construction

If we were to ask Maria to place these stressors into the four-quadrant chart, here is what it might look like:

Important, Can Control	Important, Cannot Control
✓ Finishing the work deadline that affects her performance review ✓ Following up with her daughter's teacher about missing assignments	✓ Her father's declining health and upcoming medical tests ✓ Economic uncertainty and rising interest rates affecting her mortgage
Not Important, Can Control	**Not Important, Cannot Control**
✗ Responding to a group text about weekend plans ✗ Checking social media notifications during work hours	✗ Traffic delays due to construction ✗ A coworker's negative attitude in the break room

Seeing her stressors sorted this way, Maria gains immediate clarity. Now, Maria might ask herself which of the stressors am I spending the most energy on. How can I shift my focus toward the important things that I can control? What boundaries or reframing strategies can I use to reduce the emotional weight of others?

Now Maria can reframe her thinking. Instead of 'I can't handle this,' she can tell herself, 'This is hard, but I'm learning.' Instead of 'Everything is falling apart,' she can recognize, 'Some things are falling into place.' And instead of 'I'm failing,' she can say, 'I'm growing through this.'

Finding your Main Thing – Values and Priorities

The quadrants show you where to focus your energy. But within Quadrant 1 (important/can control), you still have choices. You can't do everything. This is where "The Main Thing" comes in.

Keep the Main Thing the Main Thing.
(Covey)

"The Main Thing" is not your to-do list. It's not the pile of tasks waiting in your inbox or the errands scribbled on a sticky note. It's deeper than that. It's the core value, goal, or relationship that matters most to you right now, in this season of life. It's the anchor that helps you manage complexity and make decisions with clarity.

Your Main Thing might be your health, your family, your faith, your creative work, or your leadership role. It's not fixed forever; it evolves. What mattered most five years ago may not be what matters most today, and that's okay. Life changes. Priorities shift. The power lies in recognizing what matters now.

When everything feels urgent, identifying your Main Thing helps you cut through the noise. It's the lens through which you reframe your stressors. Instead of reacting to every demand, you begin to respond with intention. You ask: Does this serve my Main Thing? If the answer is yes, it gets your energy. If not, it can wait or be released entirely.

Knowing your Main Thing doesn't eliminate stress, but it organizes it. It gives you permission to say no, to delegate, to pause. It turns chaos into clarity. And in moments of overwhelm, it reminds you what truly deserves your attention.

A personal story comes to mind. A very good friend of mine, Derrick, had worked for years to climb the corporate ladder. When a C-suite role finally opened, he was the frontrunner. I always remembered him as extremely smart, and very humble about it. The promotion would mean more money, more influence, and the culmination of everything he'd worked for. But just as the interviews began, his sister's health took a sharp decline. She needed daily care, someone to manage medications, attend appointments, and simply be present. Unfortunately, he was the only other surviving member of their family.

Derrick was torn. The company offered flexibility, but the new role would demand long hours and frequent travel. He sat with the decision for days, weighing ambition against responsibility. Then he asked himself: What's my Main Thing right now?

The answer was clear: Being there for his sister.

It wasn't easy. He turned down the promotion, knowing it might not come again. But he also knew he'd never regret showing up for the person who had always shown up for him. In that season, his Main Thing was family. And choosing it brought peace, even in sacrifice.

REBT Integration: The Role of Beliefs

Rational Emotive Behavior Therapy (REBT), developed by Albert Ellis, is based on the core idea that it's not events themselves that cause stress, but rather our beliefs about those events. REBT uses the ABC Model to explain this process: an Activating event

(A) triggers a Belief (B), often irrational or unhelpful, which then leads to a Consequence (C), such as emotional distress or unproductive behavior. For example, missing a deadline (A) might lead to the belief "I'm a complete failure" (B), resulting in anxiety or avoidance (C).

REBT teaches us to challenge that belief: 'Is missing one deadline evidence of complete failure? Or is it simply a setback I can learn from?' By replacing the irrational belief with a more rational one, "I missed this deadline, but I can adjust and do better next time", the emotional consequence shifts from paralyzing anxiety to constructive problem-solving. The power of REBT lies in its emphasis on examining and challenging these beliefs. When we learn to replace rigid, extreme, or self-defeating thoughts with more rational and flexible ones, we can dramatically change our emotional responses and reduce stress even when the activating events remain the same.

How REBT Can Help You Find Your Main Thing

In a world full of competing demands, it's easy to feel pulled in every direction: work, family, community, personal goals, and the endless stream of expectations. Often, this overwhelm isn't just about having too much to do. It's about the conflicting beliefs we hold about what we should be doing, who we should be for others, and what makes us worthy. These beliefs can obscure our ability to identify and focus on what truly matters, our Main Thing.

This is where Rational Emotive Behavior Therapy (REBT), becomes a powerful tool. Using the ABC Model, let's break down a typical sequence of thoughts. First, suppose that you're asked to take on a new project at work. This is the (A) activating event. You (B) believe that if you say no, you'll be seen as lazy or uncommitted, resulting in anxiety and guilt, the (C) consequence.

When we examine and challenge these beliefs, we can change our emotional and behavioral responses even if the external situation doesn't change.

Irrational Beliefs That Obscure Your Main Thing

Many people struggle to identify their Main Thing because they're operating under a set of irrational beliefs that create internal conflict. We hear this all the time. "I must be everything to everyone." This belief leads to burnout and prevents prioritization. You can't be fully present for what matters most if you're trying to meet everyone's expectations. Another irrational belief that is commons is, "If I say no, I'm selfish, failing, or letting people down." Saying no is often necessary to protect your time, energy, and focus. REBT helps you reframe this belief to: "Saying no allows me to say yes to what matters." When is the last time that you said to yourself, "I should be able to handle it all." This perfectionistic belief ignores human limits. REBT encourages self-compassion and realistic expectations. Finally, in our get-ahead world, "My worth depends on my productivity, success, or approval" is a chorus that many sing over and over to themselves. This belief ties identity to external validation. REBT helps you separate your inherent worth from performance metrics.

The REBT Process for Clarity

Using REBT to help face life conflicts can be broken down into a straightforward process.

First, identify the conflict. Ask yourself what is pulling you in multiple directions. For example, you may find that the demands of your job are negatively impacting the time that you can spend with your family.

Next, examine your beliefs. What are you telling yourself? How are they in conflict? "If I don't work late, I'll fall behind on my project and possibly lose my job." Then, you might think, "If I miss my kid's game, I'm a bad parent."

Then, challenge the irrational beliefs. Are these absolutely true? What is the evidence? Will one missed deadline truly end your career? If you miss one game, will that permanently damage your relationship with your family?

Now, replace those irrational beliefs with rational ones. "I can set boundaries at work and still be valued." And "Being present means more than being perfect."

Finally, identify your core value. What do you believe at your deepest level? "My family relationships are my priority this season." This becomes your Main Thing.

Once you identify your Main Thing, whether it's caring for a loved one, protecting your health, deepening a relationship, or pursuing a meaningful goal, decisions become clearer. You stop reacting to every demand and start responding with intention.

Ava's story illustrates what discovering your Main Thing can do.

Ava was the go-to person for everyone, her coworkers, her friends, and her extended family. She never said no. She stayed late at work, hosted weekend gatherings, volunteered for school events, and answered texts at all hours. I'm sure you see someone you know in this story as well.

On the outside, she looked dependable. On the inside, she was exhausted. Burnout crept in slowly, masked by the belief she clung to: *"I must never disappoint anyone."*

One day, after missing her daughter's recital to attend a last-minute work meeting, Ava broke down. She began to question the belief that had been driving her choices. *Is it true that I must never disappoint anyone? Is it even possible? Is it helping me live the life I want?* Through reflection and journaling, she uncovered a deeper truth: her core value wasn't about pleasing everyone, it was about showing up authentically for the people she loves.

That became her Main Thing.

It didn't mean she stopped caring. It meant she started choosing. She said no to things that pulled her away from what mattered most. And yes: to presence, to boundaries, to being real. Some people were disappointed. But Ava wasn't. She was finally living in alignment with her values.

Practical Questions to Finding Your Main Thing

- What truly matters to me in this season of my life?
- If I could only protect one thing, what would it be?
- What am I willing to disappoint others to protect?
- What do I want to be true about my life one year from now?
- When I'm stressed, what am I afraid of losing?
- What gives my life meaning right now?

Values clarification exercise:

- List your top 5 values (family, health, creativity, service, growth, etc.)
- Rank them for THIS season (not forever)
- Your #1 is likely your Main Thing

Living Your Main Thing

How do you live your Main Thing? What does it look like? For starters, use it as a decision filter. Ask yourself, "Does this serve my Main Thing?" Have the courage to say no even to good opportunities that don't align with your Main Thing. Say yes, even when it is hard, to things that align with your Main Thing. Finally, be sure to communicate it to others so they understand your choices and the reasoning behind them. People might not agree with you, but when you present your Main Thing with clarity and resolve, they will at least understand you.

Some simple examples will provide more context. For example, if your Main Thing is recovering from an accident, you might easily say no to extra projects so you can say yes to physical therapy. You might value being present for your kids as the Main Thing, so you say no to committee assignments and yes to volunteering as your child's coach. Or you might value finishing your degree and turn down social events to prioritize time to study.

Putting it all Together

To manage stress with clarity, start by using the Four Quadrants to sort your stressors by importance and control. Focus your energy on Quadrant 1: Important & Can Control. This is where your effort has the greatest impact. Within this quadrant, apply REBT (Rational Emotive Behavior Therapy) to examine your beliefs about what matters: Are they true? Are they helpful? This reflection helps you uncover your Main Thing: the core value, goal, or relationship that matters most in your current season of life. Once you identify your Main Thing, use it as a lens for decision-making. It becomes your compass, guiding you through complexity and helping you respond to stress with purpose instead of pressure.

Common Obstacles

Identifying your Main Thing is powerful, but it's not always easy. Here are four common mental roadblocks that can cloud clarity and stall progress, along with reframes to help you move forward:

"But everything feels important!"

Yes, it feels that way but is it truly important, or just urgent? Urgency creates pressure, but not everything urgent is meaningful. Start by naming just one thing you'd protect if you could only protect one. That's likely your Main Thing. Use the Four Quadrants to sort your stressors. Ask: Does this align with my values? Will it matter in a month? A year? Prioritize what's important and within your control. Let urgency stop dictating your energy.

"What if my Main Thing hurts someone?"

Choosing your Main Thing may mean saying no, setting boundaries, or disappointing others. That's hard but necessary. You can't pour from an empty cup. Protecting your Main Thing isn't selfish, it's sustainable. When you honor what matters most, you show up more fully and authentically for the people you love over the long haul.

"What if I choose wrong?"

Your Main Thing isn't a lifelong contract, it's a reflection of what matters right now. Seasons change. Priorities shift. What's important today may evolve tomorrow, and that's okay. The goal isn't perfection, it's presence. Choosing something now gives you clarity and direction, even if you adjust later. You can always recalibrate as circumstances change. The real mistake is choosing nothing at all.

"I feel guilty saying no."

Guilt often signals growth. It means you're challenging old beliefs like "I must never disappoint anyone" or "My worth depends on being needed." Use REBT to examine these beliefs: Are they true? Are they helpful? Saying no to what drains you is saying yes to what sustains you. That's not failure, it's wisdom.

Here's a brief fictional story that might help you as you walk through the complete process.

Jordan was overwhelmed. Between work deadlines, family obligations, financial worries, and social commitments, every day felt like a sprint with no finish line. One evening, after snapping at his partner over something trivial, he realized he needed to pause and sort through the chaos.

He started by listing all his stressors. A looming presentation at work, his son struggling in school, mounting credit card debt, a friend upset he hadn't returned calls, pressure to volunteer at church, constant notifications from group chats, and his own declining energy and sleep.

Next, he sorted them into the Four Quadrants. Important & Can Control: Helping his son with school, preparing for the presentation, improving sleep. Important & Cannot Control: His son's learning challenges, the economy affecting his debt. Not Important & Can Control: Group chat distractions, overcommitting to volunteer work. Finally, Not Important & Cannot Control: Others' opinions about his availability.

Then, Jordan examined his beliefs about what "should" matter. He noticed thoughts like, "I must be available to everyone." "If I say no, I'm letting people down." "I should be able to handle all of this."

Using REBT, he challenged these beliefs by reflecting and asking himself, Is it true that I must never disappoint anyone? Is it helpful to believe my worth depends on doing everything? What belief would serve me better? Through this reflection, Jordan uncovered his Main Thing: "I want to be present and supportive for my family, especially my son, during this season."

With that clarity, he made a specific decision: He declined the volunteer request, muted the group chat, and scheduled time each evening to help his son with homework. He also blocked time to prepare for his presentation without guilt.

The result? Jordan felt lighter. His stress didn't vanish, but it became organized. He had a clear focus, and his decisions aligned with what mattered most. The noise quieted, and clarity took its place.

Reflection Worksheet: Reframing Your Stressors

Step 1: Identify Your Stressors

List the things currently causing you stress. Be honest and specific. Use more paper if you need to!

Step 2: Sort Them into the Four Quadrants

Important & Can Control

Important & Cannot Control

Not Important & Can Control

Not Important & Cannot Control

Step 3: Examine Your Beliefs

- What am I telling myself about what I "should" do/be/handle?

- Which beliefs are serving me? Which are creating unnecessary stress?

- What can I let go of to make space for what matters?

Step 4: Identifying Your "Main Thing"

What are your top 5 values right now?

In this season of my life, my "Main Thing" is:

Step 5: One Decision I'll Make Differently

Final Thoughts

Reframing doesn't mean pretending everything is fine. It means looking at your stressors through a more honest, helpful lens, one that empowers rather than overwhelms. Finding your Main Thing doesn't mean other things don't matter. It means you're choosing where to focus your limited energy, so that what matters most gets the attention it deserves.

Life will always present competing demands. But when you sort your stressors, challenge your beliefs, and identify your Main Thing, you move from reaction to intention. You stop trying to do it all and start doing what matters. Clarity is power. Focus is freedom. And in the heat of life's chaos, that's how you cool down.

Now that you know what matters most and where to focus, let's talk about how to protect it: self-care.

Self-Care Isn't Selfish

You can't pour from an empty cup. Take care of yourself first.

This feels like a Joan Rivers, "Can we talk?" moment. Hear me on this: self-care is not a luxury. It's not indulgent. It's not selfish. It's survival. It's how you stay in the game. It's how you show up for your family, your work, your community and most importantly, for yourself.

Somewhere along the way, we were taught that taking care of ourselves meant we were weak, lazy, or self-centered. That we should always put others first. That rest is earned, not essential.

That's a lie.

When I present the topic of self-care at workshops, one of the most impactful questions I ask is:

When was the last time you did something just for you?

I leave the slide on the screen, and I don't say a word for about a minute. That typically is as long as most people can handle trying to answer the question without becoming emotional. (And some still do!) The silence is typically deafening.

I'm not talking about a two-week vacation to Europe. I'm not even talking about a girls' weekend or spa day. I'm talking about stopping by a coffee shop for a less-than-drinkable, $7 cup of coffee and sitting alone with your own thoughts for 30 minutes while you read a magazine that tells you how much better other peoples' lives are!

So, dear reader, answer the question.

This chapter will explore practical, sustainable ways to care for yourself without guilt.

The Oxygen Mask Rule

If you've ever flown on a plane, you've heard the safety instructions: *"Put your own oxygen mask on first before helping others."* Why? Because you're no good to anyone if you're unconscious. The same applies to life. If you're constantly running on empty, you're not helping anyone… you're just burning out.

My wife recounts a specific time before we were married when she was exhausting herself daily. Her weekday routine would include waking up early enough to fit her exercise in before taking four kids to four different schools, going to her teaching job, working all day, picking up the four kids and delivering them to four different sports practices, or watching games, coming home to homework, laundry, and cooking dinner.

You can predict the end of the story. She ignored a nagging cough, was not taking care of her own needs, and ended up in the hospital with pneumonia.

Caring for myself is not self-indulgence; it is self-preservation. (Lorde)

So, what happens when you don't put your mask on first? When you neglect your own self-care in order to care for others, the consequences can be serious and far-reaching. Physically, your body begins to break down under the strain: chronic exhaustion, frequent illness, and even injury become more likely. Emotionally, you may feel depleted, with nothing left to give, even to those you care about most. This often leads to resentment toward the very people you're trying to help because your needs are going unmet while theirs take priority.

Over time, your effectiveness diminishes. You may still be showing up, but not at your best, making mistakes, missing cues, or offering support that's half-hearted. Perhaps most concerning, you begin to model unhealthy patterns for children, colleagues, or loved ones: teaching them, unintentionally, that burnout is noble and boundaries are optional. Putting your oxygen mask on first isn't selfish, it's essential. It's how you sustain your ability to care, lead, and love with clarity and strength.

Remember: You're not taking FROM others when you care for yourself. You're ensuring you have something TO GIVE.

Permission Granted

Many people carry invisible rules about what they're allowed to do. If that's you, hear this clearly: you have permission.

You have permission to rest even when the to-do list isn't finished. You have permission to prioritize your health, even if others don't understand. To set boundaries without explaining. To ask for help, because needing support isn't weakness; it's wisdom.

You also have permission to change your mind about commitments, relationships, and long-held beliefs. To do less. To honor your needs without apology. Your worth is not measured by your productivity, your availability, or your ability to keep everyone else comfortable.

Key message: Self-care isn't something you earn after everything else is done. It's what enables you to do everything else.

I recall a participant coming up to me after a workshop that I presented to a state association of social workers. By the nature of their work, they, along with teachers, doctors, nurses, first responders, etc., are care givers and they find self-care "taking" difficult. She was quite emotional and could hardly get the words out. "Thank you so much. I needed to hear that. Nobody ever gave me permission to take care of myself." She gained her composure and said that she had decided to stay one extra day after the conference to enjoy the mountain views and pamper herself. I was also moved realizing that here was someone who was giving life to the workshop's focus.

Boundaries – What Saying No Looks Like

Understanding the oxygen mask principle is the first step. Now let's explore the practical skill that makes it possible: boundaries.

One of the most powerful ways to care for yourself is to set boundaries. Boundaries aren't walls—they're bridges to healthier relationships. They teach others how to treat you and remind you that your needs matter too. They aren't punishments, they are protection! A common misconception is that if I set boundaries, I'm being mean/selfish/difficult. But the reality is, "If I don't set boundaries, I'm being dishonest about my capacity and building resentment."

Digital Boundaries

We live in a world where our pockets buzz with demands. The average person carries dozens of apps, each one eager to push noise into our day. Stove alerts, dryer alerts, doorbell cameras showing cats, fitness apps reminding us to stand, and random games begging for attention. Every app acts like it's the most important thing in your life. And without boundaries, your phone becomes a stress machine.

The Notification Problem

Notifications are designed to interrupt. They hijack your attention, fragment your focus, and create a false sense of urgency. But here's the truth: not everything needs your immediate response. A smoke detector alert? Yes. A notification that someone liked your photo from three days ago? No. The constant pinging trains your brain to be reactive, not intentional.

Practical Strategies for Digital Boundaries

Turn off non-essential notifications. Go through your settings and ask: Do I need this alert in real time? Most apps can wait. Determine what's truly urgent. Your calendar reminder for a meeting? Important. A flash sale on socks? Not so much. Don't let apps train you. You're allowed to respond on your own schedule. Just because it buzzed doesn't mean it's a priority.

After months of feeling constantly distracted and drained, I did a "notification audit." I turned off alerts from my appliances, security cameras, media, shopping apps, and even email. I kept what I considered the essentials: calls from family, calendar reminders, and emergency alerts. Within days, my stress level dropped. I felt more present in conversations, less reactive, and more in control of my time. What changed wasn't just my phone, it was my mindset. Here's another truth: just because your phone rings doesn't mean you have to answer it!

Social Media Boundaries

Social media can be a time killer and a comparison trap. You don't have to delete it all (though here's a radical idea: REMOVE ALL SOCIAL MEDIA!) But if that feels too extreme, start by curating intentionally. First, hack your algorithm. Unfollow accounts that don't serve your mental health. You can train your social media to follow what you truly want and like and stop suggesting more cat videos. Eliminate time killers by removing apps that you open out of habit rather than intention. Finally, limit your news exposure or at least don't let it dominate your day. Choose trusted sources and set time limits.

The Permission to Disconnect

Here's the most important part: you have permission to disconnect. Your phone doesn't own you. You can put it in another room. You can set "Do Not Disturb" hours. You can take a full day off from screens. You don't need to be available 24/7 to be valuable. In fact, stepping away is often the most powerful way to reconnect with yourself, your people, and your purpose.

Work Boundaries

How many of you do things at work that simply are not part of your job? Stop doing them. In fast-paced, collaborative environments, it's easy to fall into the trap of saying yes to everything. You want to be helpful, responsive, and a team player. But without clear boundaries, you risk becoming the go-to person for tasks that aren't yours while your own work suffers. I often use the concept of 'tasking authority' when people mention they're overwhelmed. Like many of us, I work in a structured, hierarchical organization, and everyone reports to someone. For me, I quickly say no to requests from outside my direct chain of command.

I once found myself constantly fielding requests from other divisions, you know—quick favors, 'just one thing,' 'can you take a look?' I wanted to be helpful, but these tasks were pulling me away from my core responsibilities. Eventually, I realized I was doing others' jobs while my own deadlines slipped.

I started redirecting requests through my manager. The shift was subtle but powerful. I still collaborated, but with clarity and boundaries. When people knew they had to involve my manager first, they thought twice about what they were asking.

The Cost of Not Setting Boundaries

When you don't set boundaries at work, the consequences pile up. You do others' jobs while your own work suffers, you feel resentment toward colleagues who keep asking, you burn out from overcommitment, and your quality drops across everything you touch. Remember, boundaries aren't barriers, they're filters. They help you protect your energy and deliver your best work.

What Saying No at Work Sounds Like

Saying no doesn't have to be harsh. It can be clear, kind, and professional. "I'd like to help, but I'm at capacity this week. Can we revisit next month?" Or "Let me check with my manager about priorities before committing." Try this: "I'm not the right person for this, but have you tried [appropriate person]?"

These phrases communicate respect while reinforcing your limits. They also model healthy boundaries for others.

Personal/Family Boundaries

On a personal note, I don't go to family reunions. Sure, I do get invited, I just politely decline the invitation. I'll get emails from distant first cousins asking me to come, but why? For me, I really didn't enjoy my childhood interactions with some of my extended family, so why, as an adult, should I continue them? It removes any stress of awkward questions, travel expenses, requesting time off work, and, I have other things that bring me more joy. Before you chastise me, I do keep in touch with some.

One of the most liberating truths in adult life is this: you get to choose your relationships. Not all family connections need to be maintained. Just because someone shares your DNA doesn't mean they're entitled to your time, energy, or emotional availability. Toxic relationships don't get a pass because of bloodlines. You can love someone from a distance. You can forgive without re-engaging. You can honor your own peace without guilt.

Setting boundaries with family is often the hardest because the expectations run deep. But boundaries aren't about punishment; they're about protection. They protect your mental health, your time, and your ability to show up well for the people who matter most.

Parenting Boundaries: The Power of Natural Consequences

Boundaries aren't just for adults, they're essential in parenting. Children learn responsibility through **natural and immediate consequences**, not constant rescue. One of the clearest examples: *Frank Junior forgot his glove? He can sit on the bench next time.* That moment teaches more than a lecture ever could. And for parents, letting natural consequences do the teaching is its own form of self-care—you're not constantly rescuing, managing, or stressing about things your child can learn to handle themselves.

When parents constantly bail kids out, they unintentionally teach helplessness and entitlement. Boundaries say: I love you enough to let you learn. A well-placed "no" isn't harsh, it's a gift. It builds resilience, accountability, and confidence.

What Personal Boundaries Look Like

Personal boundaries are the quiet decisions that protect your energy and well-being. They often look like limiting time with draining people, not attending every event you're invited to, saying no to hosting when you're exhausted, protecting your weekends and evenings, and choosing quality time over obligation.

These boundaries don't make you selfish, they make you sustainable. They allow you to show up with intention, not resentment.

Story: Setting a Difficult Family Boundary

After years of listening to my father's negative views about the world and everyone in it, I had a frank conversation that turned out to be our last. We disagreed on fundamental things, and every interaction left me feeling diminished—less confident, less worthy, less like myself.

So, I made a decision: in order to move forward with my life, I had to step back from our relationship. For the last three years of his life, we didn't speak. That choice wasn't easy, and it wasn't made lightly. But it was necessary. I had to protect my peace. I had to choose myself. I don't regret it. Sometimes self-preservation requires difficult boundaries, even with family.

Boundaries protect your energy by helping you say no. But self-care isn't just about what you decline, it's also about what you accept: support, help, partnership. Let's talk about asking for help and sharing the load.

Delegating and Asking for Help

Asking for help should be simple. But for many of us, it's anything but. We hesitate, delay, or avoid it altogether, often for reasons rooted in pride, fear, or habit. Here are some of the most common barriers:

"I should be able to handle this myself" assumes that needing help is failure. But you're human with limits. Needing help isn't a flaw, it's reality. No one is meant to carry everything alone.

Thinking that "everyone else is busy too" ignores the fact that, yes, people are busy, but they also want to help. Helping others creates connection and purpose and invites them into meaningful contribution.

The belief that, "If I ask for help, I'm weak, failing, or burdensome" confuses vulnerability with weakness. Asking for help is a sign of wisdom and self-awareness and shows you know your limits.

Trying to convince yourself that, "It's faster to just do it myself" maybe works in the short term. But doing everything yourself leads to burnout, which slows you down in the long run. Delegating or sharing the load creates sustainability.

Finally, believing that "No one can do it as well as I can" is foolish. Perfectionism is a trap. Letting go of control allows others to grow and frees you to focus on what truly matters. In fact, I have found that the tasks I delegate often are completed more quickly and at a higher level of quality than I would have produced.

The truth is, asking for help is a form of self-care. It's how we stay grounded, connected, and effective. You don't have to earn the right to rest or prove your strength by suffering in silence. You have permission to ask. And when you do, you'll often find that support is closer, and more willing, than you think.

People love to help. Don't abuse them and don't jeopardize their own work, but delegating tasks to others on your team can greatly reduce your own workload and leverage your time to focus on those things that *you* do best. P.S. As a manager, it gives you a chance to do a public shout-out to that person for being a great team player. People also love recognition.

Ask for Help in Your Personal Life

You don't have to do it all. You were never meant to.

In our personal lives, asking for help can feel vulnerable and even uncomfortable. We worry about being a burden, appearing weak, or disrupting others' routines. But the truth is, asking for help is one of the most human, courageous things we can do. It's how we stay connected, supported, and emotionally healthy.

Here's what asking for help might look like in everyday life. Asking a neighbor, "Can you pick up the kids Tuesday? I have a doctor's appointment." Or suggesting to your family, "I'm overwhelmed. Can we order takeout this week?" On a more personal note, you might ask, "I need to talk. Do you have 20 minutes?" Finally, find the courage to ask, "I can't host this year. Can someone else take Thanksgiving?"

These aren't signs of failure. They're signs of self-awareness. They say, "I know my limits, and I trust you enough to share them."

When Asking Made All the Difference

When my cousin Lisa's husband had a sudden medical emergency, she was thrown into crisis mode: hospital visits, paperwork, and caring for their two young kids. At first, she tried to manage everything alone. But exhaustion hit hard. Finally, she reached out to neighbors: one picked up groceries, another drove the kids to school, and a third sat with her at the hospital. That moment of asking changed everything. She felt held, not alone. Her community didn't just help, they rallied.

The Reciprocity Principle

Here's the beautiful truth: when you ask for help, you give others the gift of being needed. People want to help. It deepens relationships, builds trust, and reminds us that we're not meant to do life alone. Letting others support you isn't weakness, it's wisdom. And it often opens the door for them to ask for help when they need it, too.

You don't have to wait until you're drowning. You have permission to ask. And when you do, you'll often find that love shows up in ways you never expected.

Professional Help

Sometimes, the support we need goes beyond what friends, family, or self-help tools can offer. That's when it's time to consider professional help, from therapists, counselors, or coaches who are trained to guide you through emotional, mental, and behavioral challenges. There is no shame in seeking support. In fact, it's one of the strongest, most self-aware choices you can make.

Asking for help isn't giving up. It's refusing to give up. (Mackesy)

Common Barriers and Reality Checks

Don't let your mind tell you that, "It's too expensive." Many workplaces offer EAP (Employee Assistance Programs) with free sessions. There are also sliding scale therapists, community mental health centers, and online platforms with affordable options.

"I don't have time" is certainly not a good excuse for denying yourself the help of a professional. Virtual therapy makes it easier than ever to fit support into your schedule. Even brief, solution-focused sessions can make a meaningful difference.

Are you worried about what people will think? Your mental health matters more than others' opinions. Seeking help is not a weakness, it's a commitment to your well-being.

Finally, thinking that "I should be able to handle this myself" is not helpful at all. You see a doctor for physical health. You can see a therapist for mental health. Both are healthcare. Both are valid. You don't have to wait until you're in crisis.

You Deserve Support

Whether you're navigating grief, anxiety, burnout, relationship stress, or simply feeling stuck, professional help can offer clarity, tools, and healing. You don't have to carry it alone. You have permission to seek support. And when you do, you take a powerful step toward peace, resilience, and growth.

Do What Brings You Joy

We often think of self-care as something we do to avoid collapse: resting when we're exhausted, saying no when we're overwhelmed, setting boundaries to protect our energy. And yes, those are essential. But self-care isn't just about survival. It's also about feeding your soul. It's about reconnecting with what lights you up, what makes you feel alive, what reminds you that life is more than tasks and responsibilities.

Joy is not a distraction. It's medicine.

Reconnecting with What You Love

Here's a question worth asking: When was the last time you did something simply because you *wanted* to? Not because you had to. Not because someone else wanted you to. Not because it was on your to-do list. Just because it brought you joy.

Many of us have lost touch with that feeling. We've become so focused on productivity, obligation, and efficiency that we've forgotten how to play, how to create, how to enjoy. But joy is a form of nourishment. It restores what stress depletes. It reconnects us to our creativity, our purpose, and our humanity.

Common Activities That Feed the Soul

Joy doesn't have to be grand or expensive. It often lives in small, everyday moments: taking a walk in nature, playing or making music, creating art with your hands, dancing in your kitchen. It might be writing in a journal, building or fixing something, reading purely for pleasure. Or it could be playing with your kids or pets, laughing until your stomach hurts, cooking a meal you love. These aren't distractions from 'real life.' They are real life. They're the moments that make the rest of it worth living.

Joy Is a Form of Self-Care

When you prioritize joy, you're not being indulgent, you're being wise. You're choosing to refill your emotional tank so you can show up more fully in every area of your life. You're choosing to live, not just function.

So, give yourself permission to do what brings you joy. Schedule it. Protect it. Celebrate it. Whether it's five minutes or a full afternoon, joy is a worthy investment. Because when you feel joy, you remember who you are. And that's the most powerful kind of self-care there is.

I vividly remember a story from childhood, and it haunts me to this day as to why I don't do stuff like this more often. My three sisters and I were all ready for school, and it was time to leave. Education was important to our family, and we were not allowed to skip school, not do our homework, or be in even the least amount of disciplinary trouble. Our mother was driving yet we noticed that we were not taking the route that would get us there on time. I hated to be late, so I had to ask what we were doing going in the wrong direction. The only reply I got was a "Just wait and see." I'm not sure what inspired my mother that day, but I'm certainly glad it did. We were supposed to do the responsible thing and go to school, instead, we did the joyful thing and spent the entire day at the circus! The moral of that story: Sometimes the most important thing is to break the rules you've set for yourself and choose delight.

Go Play Outside

Nature is one of the most underrated forms of therapy. Fresh air, sunlight, movement… it all helps regulate your nervous system and restore your sense of calm. Sometimes the most powerful form of self-care is the simplest: step outside. Fresh air, sunlight, and movement aren't just pleasant, they're therapeutic. They help regulate your nervous system, calm your racing thoughts, and reconnect you to something bigger than your to-do list. Nature has a way of reminding you to breathe, to slow down, to be present.

Even **10** minutes outside can make a difference. A walk around the block, sitting under a tree, or watching the clouds shift overhead can reset your mood and restore your sense of calm. Sunlight boosts your vitamin D and improves your sleep cycle. Movement, whether it's a hike, a stretch, or just wandering, releases tension stored in your body. And the natural world, with its quiet rhythms and beauty, gently pulls you out of your head and back into your senses.

You don't need a mountain trail or a forest retreat. Your backyard, a local park, or a patch of grass will do. The goal isn't productivity, it's presence. So go play outside. Let nature do what it does best: heal, restore, and remind you that you're part of something peaceful and alive.

So… **STOP**. Put this book down. Go outside and come back when you've calmed down!

I've previously mentioned that my wife is a runner which gets her outside even on the coldest of days. She will use the treadmill to avoid the extreme heat or lightning storms, but she finds that running connects her to nature in a very spiritual way.

I tell people I don't hunt, fish, or play golf—I garden. On nice long summer days, I easily spend 10 or more hours in the garden. Whether it's mowing the lawn, planting onions, or harvesting tomatoes, I feel a connection with God in my lawn and gardens stronger than anywhere else. It heals me and restores my soul!

Permission to Play

One of the quiet tragedies of adulthood is that we forget how to play. Everything becomes productive, purposeful, or goal oriented. We stop doing things "just because," and start measuring every activity by its outcome. Play begins to feel frivolous and something reserved for children or rare vacations.

But here's the truth: play is essential. It's how we process stress, connect with others, and remember who we are beyond our roles and responsibilities. Play invites spontaneity, creativity, and laughter back into our lives. It's not a waste of time. It's a way to reclaim it.

For adults, play takes many forms. It might be board games with friends, pick-up basketball or frisbee in the park. It could be coloring books or doodling, building LEGOs or working on puzzles. Maybe it's trying a new recipe just for fun, learning an instrument, or dancing in your living room. Whatever brings you joy, without pressure, without performance, is worth doing. You have permission to play. Not because it's productive, but because it's human.

Self-Care in Practice: What it is and isn't

Self-care is often misunderstood. It's not just about bubble baths, spa days, or treating yourself after a long week, though those things can be lovely. At its core, self-care is about sustainability. It's the ongoing practice of protecting your energy, honoring your needs, and living in a way that supports your well-being. It's how you stay grounded, emotionally available, and resilient, not just for yourself, but for the people who depend on you.

True self-care means setting boundaries that protect your time and energy, even when it's uncomfortable. It means saying no to commitments, conversations, or environments that leave you depleted, and saying yes to the things that restore you whether that's solitude, creativity, movement, or connection. It means asking for help when you need it, without guilt or apology, and resting before your body forces you to. It's choosing joy, even in small doses, and treating yourself with the same compassion you offer others.

Self-care is not selfish. It's not indulgent. And it's certainly not something you earn only after everything else is done. It's not a one-size-fits-all checklist, and it's not a one-time fix. Self-care is personal. It's daily. And it's essential.

You don't have to overhaul your life to begin. Start small. Choose one boundary to set this week, perhaps turning off work notifications after dinner or declining an invitation that feels more draining than energizing. Ask for help with one thing, even if it's just a ride, a favor, or a listening ear. Do one thing that brings you joy, whether it's dancing in your kitchen, reading a chapter of a book, or sitting quietly with a cup of tea. Take one 10-minute walk and let the fresh air remind you that you're allowed to pause.

These small steps matter. One boundary leads to another. One moment of joy reminds you why it's worth protecting. One act of self-compassion opens the door to healing. Over time, these choices shape a life that's not just functional but fulfilling.

Reflection Prompt

Take a moment to answer these questions:

- What does self-care look like for me?
- What's one thing I can do this week that brings me joy?
- Where in my life do I need to set a boundary?
- Who can I ask for help right now?
- What am I saying yes to that I should say no to?
- What am I saying no to that I should say yes to?
- What would I do with an hour of completely unscheduled time?
- What would change in my life if I truly believed I deserved rest and joy?

Instruction: Write your answers down. Post them somewhere visible. Let them be your reminder that you matter too.

Self-Care Checklist: Refuel Your Mind, Body & Spirit

Check off as you complete.

Daily Self-Care

- ❏ I drank enough water today.
- ❏ I ate nourishing meals.
- ❏ I moved my body (walk, stretch, exercise).
- ❏ I took a few minutes to breathe or be still.
- ❏ I got outside or opened a window for fresh air.
- ❏ I said something kind to myself.

Emotional Self-Care

- ❏ I acknowledged how I'm feeling without judgment.
- ❏ I set a boundary or said "no" when needed.
- ❏ I asked for help or support.
- ❏ I did something that made me smile or laugh.
- ❏ I gave myself permission to rest.

Mental Self-Care

- ❏ I took a break from screens or social media.
- ❏ I journaled or reflected on my thoughts.
- ❏ I focused on one task at a time.
- ❏ I practiced gratitude or mindfulness.
- ❏ I reminded myself: "I am doing the best I can."

Connection & Joy

- ❑ I connected with someone I trust.
- ❑ I spent time doing something I love.
- ❑ I played, created, or explored something new.
- ❑ I laughed or found joy in a small moment.
- ❑ I celebrated a small win.

My Self-Care Intention for This Week:

Bringing it all Together

You've learned that self-care isn't selfish, it's survival. You've been given permission to put your oxygen mask on first, to protect your energy, and to prioritize your well-being without guilt. You've explored the power of boundaries, the importance of asking for help, and the joy that comes from reconnecting with what lights you up. And now, you have tools you can begin using today.

The truth is you don't have to do it all. You just have to start. One boundary. One moment of rest. One joyful activity. One step toward honoring yourself.

Self-care isn't just about you, it's how you show up for the people you love. It's how you sustain your work, your relationships, and your purpose. And most importantly, it's how you honor the life you've been given.

Now that you understand the importance of caring for yourself, let's explore specific practices that support both body and mind: mindfulness and mental clarity.

Mindfulness and Mental Clarity

The present moment is the only time over which we have dominion. (Thích Nhất Hạnh)

Our minds are rarely quiet. Even when our bodies are still, our thoughts race: replaying yesterday's conversations, rehearsing tomorrow's meetings, juggling mental to-do lists, worrying about things we can't control. This constant mental chatter is exhausting. It pulls us out of the present and scatters our attention across a thousand invisible threads.

Imagine someone sitting at the dinner table with their family. The food is warm, the conversation is light, and laughter fills the room. But mentally, they're somewhere else: reviewing work emails, planning tomorrow's schedule, stressing over finances. They nod and smile, but they're not *really* there. Their body is present, but their mind is miles away.

This is the cost of mental clutter. We lose the moment we're in while chasing moments that haven't happened yet or reliving ones that already have.

The Cost of Mental Clutter

When your mind is constantly busy, clarity becomes elusive. Decisions feel heavier, slower, more complicated. You second-guess yourself, overthink simple choices, and struggle to prioritize. Stress doesn't just linger, it compounds. You're not just dealing with what's happening now; you're also carrying the weight of past regrets and future fears.

And the toll isn't just emotional, it's physical. Mental overload can lead to headaches, muscle tension, digestive issues, and chronic fatigue. Your body feels what your mind carries. The more cluttered your thoughts, the harder it becomes to rest, focus, and feel present.

You miss the quiet joys right in front of you. The smile from a loved one. The warmth of sunlight on your skin. The satisfaction of a deep breath. These moments are easy to overlook when your mind is always somewhere else.

What This Chapter Offers

This chapter isn't about achieving a perfectly blank mind. That's not realistic. And it's not the goal. Instead, we'll explore how to create space between stimulus and response. How to notice what's happening in your mind without being swept away by it. How to gently return to the present, repeatedly, with compassion.

You'll learn practical tools for cultivating mental clarity, tools that work in real life, not just on mountaintops. These practices are simple, accessible, and designed to meet you where you are, whether you're in a quiet room or a chaotic day.

In a world that constantly demands our attention, mindfulness is a radical act of self-care. It's how we reclaim our focus, restore our peace, and reconnect with what matters. Let's explore what mindfulness really means and how to practice it in ways that bring clarity, calmness, and presence to your everyday life.

Mindfulness and Mental Clarity: What It Is and What It Isn't

Common Misconceptions About Mindfulness

Mindfulness is often misunderstood, especially in a culture that prizes productivity and quick fixes. Let's start by clearing up some of the most common myths.

Myth 1: "Mindfulness means clearing your mind of all thoughts."

This is one of the biggest misconceptions. The truth is, thoughts will come because that's what minds do. Mindfulness isn't about stopping your thoughts; it's about noticing them without getting tangled in them. Imagine your thoughts as clouds drifting across the sky. You don't try to stop the clouds; you simply watch them pass. That's mindfulness: observing without attachment.

Myth 2: "You have to sit cross-legged on a mountaintop."

Mindfulness doesn't require a special setting or ritual. You can practice it while washing dishes, waiting in line, walking to your car, or sitting at your desk. It's not about where you are, it's about how you pay attention. Everyday moments are perfect opportunities to be present.

Myth 3: "Mindfulness will make you feel calm and peaceful all the time."

While mindfulness can lead to greater calm, it's not a guarantee of serenity. Sometimes, being present means facing uncomfortable emotions you've been avoiding. That's not failure, it's awareness. The goal isn't constant peace; it's honest presence. And sometimes, presence means sitting with discomfort until it passes.

Myth 4: "It's a religious practice."

Mindfulness has roots in Buddhist tradition, but the practice itself is secular and accessible to anyone. It's simply about paying attention. Many religious traditions have their own contemplative practices: Christian contemplative prayer, Jewish meditation, Islamic dhikr, but mindfulness, as taught in modern psychology and wellness, is open to all, regardless of belief system.

Myth 5: "It takes too much time."

Mindfulness doesn't require hours of silence or retreat. Even 60 seconds of intentional breathing counts. You don't need a perfect schedule, you need consistency. A few minutes a day can begin to shift your relationship with stress, attention, and emotion.

What Mindfulness Actually Is

So, what *is* mindfulness?

At its core, mindfulness is paying attention to the present moment, to what's happening inside you and around you, without judgment, without trying to fix it, and without getting lost in it. It's a practice of awareness, acceptance, and intentional focus.

Let's break that down:

Present-moment awareness means noticing what's happening *right now*. Not ruminating on the past. Not worrying about the future. Just being here, in this moment, with whatever is unfolding. It could be the sound of your breath, the feeling of your feet on the ground, or the emotion rising in your chest.

Non-judgment is the practice of observing your thoughts and feelings without labeling them as "good" or "bad." Instead of saying, "I shouldn't feel anxious," mindfulness invites you to say, "I notice I'm feeling anxious." That shift creates space for compassion and clarity.

Intentional attention means choosing where to focus, rather than being pulled in every direction by distractions. It's active, not passive. You're training your mind to stay with what matters, even when it wants to wander.

Acceptance is the ability to acknowledge reality as it is, without resistance. That doesn't mean giving up, it means seeing clearly so you can respond wisely. Acceptance isn't resignation; it's the foundation for meaningful action.

The Space Between Stimulus and Response

One of the most powerful gifts of mindfulness is the ability to create space between what happens and how you respond. As Viktor Frankl wrote:

"Between stimulus and response there is a space. In that space is our power to choose our response. In our response lies our growth and our freedom."

Mindfulness gives you access to that space. It's the pause that allows you to respond instead of react. It's the breath before the reply, the moment of clarity before the decision, the awareness that lets you choose compassion over defensiveness, patience over frustration, presence over distraction.

In the pages ahead, we'll explore how to cultivate this space in your daily life. You'll learn simple, practical tools for mental clarity, tools that don't require silence or perfection, just a willingness to show up and pay attention.

What Mindfulness Does for You

Mindfulness isn't just a calming practice, it's a transformative one. When you begin to pay attention to the present moment with intention and without judgment, you start to experience real shifts in how you think, feel, and relate to the world around you.

Mental Benefits

One of the first changes people notice is a reduction in mental clutter. Mindfulness helps quiet the constant loop of rumination and overthinking. Instead of spiraling through "what ifs" and worst-case scenarios, you learn to anchor yourself in "what is." This clarity improves focus and concentration, making it easier to complete tasks and make decisions. Over time, mindfulness also helps you recognize unhelpful thought patterns, like catastrophizing, perfectionism, or black-and-white thinking, and gently interrupt them before they take over.

Emotional Benefits

Emotionally, mindfulness brings you back from the edge. It reduces anxiety by shifting your attention from imagined futures to the reality of the present. You begin to observe your emotions without being controlled by them. You might notice, *"I'm feeling overwhelmed,"* instead of becoming overwhelmed. This space between feeling and reacting builds emotional resilience. It also creates room for self-compassion, allowing you to treat yourself with kindness, even when you're struggling.

Physical Benefits

The body responds to mindfulness, too. Studies show that regular practice can lower cortisol levels, the hormone associated with stress. It can reduce blood pressure, improve sleep quality, and help release physical tension that builds up from chronic stress. Even a few minutes of mindful breathing can signal your nervous system to shift from fight-or-flight into rest-and-digest.

Relational Benefits

Mindfulness also transforms relationships. When you're present, you actually listen. You're less reactive, more thoughtful, and more attuned to others' emotions. This reduces misunderstandings and conflict, especially those born from defensiveness or distraction. You begin to respond with intention rather than impulse, creating deeper, more meaningful connections.

A Real-Life Example

Consider this: A parent used to come home from work feeling frazzled and short-tempered. They'd walk through the door and immediately snap at their kids over noise, mess, or minor things. Then they started taking two minutes in the car before coming inside. Just two minutes of breathing, noticing, and resetting. That small act of mindfulness completely changed their evenings. They walked in calmer, more present, and more able to connect.

Or think of someone who catches themselves spiraling into worst-case thinking, *"What if I lose my job? What if everything falls apart?"* Instead of following the spiral, they pause, breathe, and ask, *"What's actually happening right now?"* That moment of mindfulness doesn't erase the fear, but it grounds them in reality—and that's where clarity begins.

Mindfulness isn't magic. It's a practice. But over time, it becomes a powerful tool for mental clarity, emotional balance, physical well-being, and deeper relationships. And it all starts with a single breath.

Simple Practices for Everyday Life

Mindfulness isn't something you master, it's something you practice.

It's not about perfection or enlightenment. It's about presence. And the good news is, you don't need hours of silence or a retreat in the mountains to begin. You can start today, right where you are, with simple techniques that fit into your life.

Practice 1: Breath Awareness (The Foundation)

Breathing is the foundation of mindfulness because it's always with you. No matter where you are or what you're doing, your breath is a built-in anchor to the present moment. Intentional breathing activates your parasympathetic nervous system, the part of your body responsible for calming you down. It's your reset button.

To begin, find a comfortable position. You can sit, stand, or lie down. Close your eyes or soften your gaze. Then, simply notice your breath. Don't try to change it, just observe. Feel the air entering your nose, filling your lungs, and leaving your body. When your mind wanders (and it will), gently bring your attention back to your breath.

There's no judgment here. Your mind may wander dozens of times. That's not failure, it's practice. Each time you return to your breath, you strengthen your ability to be present.

For moments of acute stress, try Box Breathing, a structured technique used by military personnel, first responders, and athletes to regulate their nervous systems:

1. Breathe in for 4 counts
2. Hold for 4 counts

3. Breathe out for 4 counts
4. Hold for 4 counts
5. Repeat 4–5 times

This simple rhythm can calm your body and clear your mind in just a few minutes.

Practice 2: The 5-4-3-2-1 Grounding Exercise

When anxiety hits or your thoughts start spiraling, the 5-4-3-2-1 technique can bring you back to the present moment. It's a sensory-based grounding exercise that helps you reconnect with your body and surroundings.

Here's how it works:

Notice 5 things you can see. Look around—what's in your environment? A coffee mug, a tree, your hands, a book, the clock on the wall.

Notice 4 things you can touch. The texture of your shirt, the smooth surface of your phone, the ground beneath your feet, the cool air on your skin.

Notice 3 things you can hear. Traffic outside, a clock ticking, your own breathing, distant voices.

Notice 2 things you can smell. Coffee, soap on your hands, fresh air, a candle.

Notice 1 thing you can taste. The lingering flavor of lunch, mint toothpaste, or simply the inside of your mouth.

This exercise interrupts the loop of anxious thinking and brings you back to what's real—not imagined, not feared, but present.

Example:

Before a big presentation, Maya felt her chest tighten and her thoughts race. She remembered the 5-4-3-2-1 technique and gave it a try. She named five things she could see in the conference room, felt the cool table under her hands, listened to the hum of the projector, noticed the scent of her coffee, and focused on the taste of her breath mint. Within minutes, her heart rate slowed, and she felt grounded enough to begin. The presentation went well, but more importantly, she now had a tool she could trust.

Practice 3: Mindful Moments (Integrating Mindfulness into Daily Life)

You don't need to carve out extra time for mindfulness. You can turn everyday activities into moments of presence. The key is to do one thing at a time—with your full attention.

Mindful eating is a great place to start. Instead of rushing through meals or eating while scrolling your phone, slow down. Notice the colors, smells, and textures of your food. Chew slowly. Taste fully. Put your fork down between bites. This isn't about eating perfectly, it's about being present with your food.

Mindful walking is another simple practice. As you walk, feel your feet touching the ground. Notice the rhythm of your steps. Observe your surroundings: the trees, the sky, the sounds. Let your thoughts come and go without following them.

Even chores can become mindfulness practices. Mindful dishwashing means feeling the warm water on your hands, noticing the texture of the soap and dishes, and listening to the sounds around you. What was once a task becomes a moment of calm.

Mindful showering is my favorite. Feel the water temperature on your skin. Notice the scent of your shampoo. Listen to the sound of the water. Let the shower be a reset, not just a routine.

The principle is simple: Whatever you're doing, be fully there. That's mindfulness.

Practice 4: Body Scan (Releasing Physical Tension)

Stress doesn't just live in your mind, it lives in your body. A body scan helps you notice and release physical tension, reconnecting you with yourself.

This practice is especially helpful before bed, when you feel disconnected from your body, or when you notice tightness or discomfort.

To begin, lie down or sit comfortably and close your eyes. Start at the top of your head and slowly move your attention downward. Notice sensations, warmth, coolness, tension, tingling. Move through your forehead, eyes, jaw, neck, shoulders, arms, chest, stomach, hips, legs, and feet.

When you find tension, breathe into it. Don't try to force it away, just observe. If your mind wanders, gently guide it back to the body part you're scanning.

Benefits of a mental body scan include an increased awareness of where you hold stress (tight shoulders, clenched jaw), release of unconscious tension, improved sleep quality, and a deeper connection to your physical self.

When my wife was hit by the truck, and at many other times of injury, she will go through a mental body check. Literally. She begins with her head and works her way all the way down to her individual toes. It helps her to listen to her body, and it is a practice that has not failed her yet!

Practice 5: Thought Observation (Noticing Without Engaging)

One of the most powerful shifts mindfulness offers is the ability to observe your thoughts without believing or obeying them. We often assume that every thought we have is true, urgent, or meaningful. But thoughts are just mental events, not facts, not commands.

Imagine your thoughts as leaves floating down a stream. They appear, they drift, and they pass. You don't have to grab them. You don't have to follow them.

To practice, sit quietly and notice when a thought arises. Label it simply: "thinking," "worrying," "planning." Let it pass. Return to your breath.

Example:

A thought arises: "I'm going to fail this presentation."

Instead of spiraling, you notice: "I'm having the thought that I might fail."

This creates distance. It's just a thought, not a prophecy.

Another thought: "I can't handle this."

You observe: "I'm having the thought that I can't handle this."

Then ask: "Is that true? Or is that fear talking?"

This practice helps you recognize patterns, challenge distortions, and respond with clarity. You are not your thoughts. You are the awareness that observes them.

Final Thought

Mindfulness doesn't require perfection. It requires practice. These simple techniques, breath awareness, grounding, mindful moments, body scans, and thought observation, are tools you can use anytime, anywhere. They don't demand silence or stillness. They ask only for your attention.

Start where you are. One breath. One moment. One step toward clarity.

Mindfulness practices are accessible to everyone, but for many people, spiritual or contemplative practices offer an additional layer of meaning, connection, and peace. Whether you call it prayer, meditation, or simply sitting in silence, these practices have sustained humanity for thousands of years.

Prayer, Meditation, and Contemplative Practices

Common Ground Between Mindfulness and Spirituality

Across cultures and traditions, contemplative practices have long served as gateways to presence, stillness, and awareness. Whether rooted in religious devotion or secular introspection, these practices invite us to pause, breathe, and reconnect with ourselves and with something greater than ourselves.

At their core, both mindfulness and spirituality offer a reprieve from the relentless pace of modern life. They encourage us to step away from constant doing and achieving, and instead embrace being. This shared emphasis on presence fosters a deep sense of connection whether one calls it God, Spirit, the Universe, or simply the interconnectedness of all life.

In this way, mindfulness and spirituality are not opposing forces but complementary paths. They both build inner stillness, open-hearted awareness, and a sense of belonging to something beyond the self.

Respecting Different Paths

One of the most beautiful aspects of contemplative practice is its diversity. You don't have to be religious to meditate, and you don't have to meditate to pray. These practices can stand alone or enrich each other. What matters most is authenticity, finding what resonates with your heart and soul.

For some, prayer is a lifeline to divine presence. For others, meditation is a way to quiet the mind and listen inwardly. Some blend both, using breathwork to enter prayer or scripture to guide meditation. There is no single "right" way, only the way that brings you closer to peace, clarity, and connection.

Prayer as Mindfulness

Prayer, often seen as a spiritual act, can also be a deeply mindful one. It offers a space to externalize thoughts, fears, and hopes, and to seek comfort, guidance, and peace. When approached contemplatively, prayer becomes less about asking and more about resting in presence.

Centering Prayer (Christian Tradition)

This practice involves choosing a sacred word such as *peace*, *grace*, or *Jesus*, and sitting in silence. When the mind wanders, gently return to the word. It's not about petitioning God but about being with God. Much like mantra meditation, centering prayer anchors the mind and opens the heart.

The Jesus Prayer (Orthodox Tradition)

"Lord Jesus Christ, have mercy on me." This simple phrase is repeated slowly and rhythmically, often in sync with the breath. Over time, it becomes a heartbeat of presence, aligning mind and spirit.

Lectio Divina (Sacred Reading)

This ancient practice involves reading a short passage of scripture slowly and reflectively. One listens for a word or phrase that stands out, sits with it, and responds with prayer or contemplation. It's a way of letting sacred texts speak directly to the soul.

Gratitude Prayer

Gratitude is a powerful doorway to mindfulness. Simply naming what you're thankful for: sunlight on your face, a kind word, a warm meal, grounds you in the present moment and shifts your focus from scarcity to abundance.

Example: Consider someone who struggled with traditional prayer, feeling disconnected or unsure of what to say. Upon discovering centering prayer, they found peace in silence, realizing that presence itself could be prayer. Or someone who began each day by listing three things they were grateful for and noticed a profound shift in their mood and perspective.

Meditation Practices

Meditation is often associated with Eastern traditions, but its benefits are universal. It cultivates mental stillness, emotional regulation, and connection to inner wisdom. Like prayer, it's a practice of returning repeatedly to the present moment.

Breath-Focused Meditation

This foundational practice involves simply observing the breath. Inhale, exhale. When the mind wanders, gently return to the breath. It's deceptively simple, yet profoundly effective in calming the nervous system and sharpening awareness.

Loving-Kindness Meditation (Metta)

This practice involves silently repeating phrases of goodwill: "May I be safe. May I be healthy. May I be at peace." These wishes are extended to loved ones, strangers, and even those we struggle with. It's a powerful way to create compassion and dissolve resentment.

Mantra Meditation

Repeating a word or phrase, such as *Om*, *peace*, or *I am enough*, helps anchor the mind and quiet inner chatter. The repetition becomes a rhythm, a sacred pulse that draws us inward.

Walking Meditation

Mindfulness doesn't require stillness. In walking meditation, each step becomes a moment of awareness. You feel the ground beneath your feet, the rhythm of your movement, the air on your skin. It's a moving prayer, practiced in Buddhist traditions and accessible to all.

Guided Meditation

For beginners, guided meditation can offer structure and support. Apps like Insight Timer, Calm, and Headspace, or free recordings on YouTube, provide a variety of practices, from body scans to visualizations, to help you get started.

Contemplative Practices Across Traditions

Mindfulness and spirituality are not confined to any one religion or philosophy. Across the world, cultures have developed practices that reflect the universal human longing for connection and peace.

Jewish Meditation

In Judaism, Hitbodedut involves spontaneous, personal conversation with God, often in nature. Breath prayers tied to Hebrew words and contemplation of Torah passages also serve as meditative practices.

Islamic Practices

Dhikr, the remembrance of God, involves repeating divine names or phrases, often with rhythmic breathing or movement. In Sufism, whirling becomes a form of moving meditation, symbolizing spiritual ascent and surrender.

Hindu Practices

Japa, the repetition of mantras, is central to Hindu meditation. Yoga, originally a spiritual discipline, combines breath, movement, and focus. Practices may also involve visualization of chakras or the third eye.

Secular Mindfulness

Developed by Jon Kabat-Zinn, Mindfulness-Based Stress Reduction (MBSR) removes religious language to make mindfulness accessible to all. It's taught in hospitals, schools, and workplaces, backed by scientific research showing its benefits for stress, anxiety, and overall well-being.

The Universal Thread: Whether through prayer, meditation, movement, or silence, these practices share a common goal: to quiet the mind, open the heart, and cultivate presence.

How to Begin Practice

Starting a contemplative practice doesn't require hours of free time or a mountaintop retreat. It begins with small, intentional steps.

Start Small

Just 2–5 minutes a day can make a difference. Consistency matters more than duration. Many find mornings easiest, before the day's demands take over.

Create a Simple Space

You don't need a meditation room. A quiet corner, a chair by a window, a cushion, or a candle can create a sacred space. What matters is intention.

Choose What Resonates

Try different practices. Notice what feels natural and what feels forced. It's okay if prayer feels right and meditation doesn't, or vice versa. You can mix and match: breathwork followed by gratitude prayer, or scripture reading followed by silent reflection.

Be Patient With Yourself

Your mind will wander. That's not failure, it's practice. Some days will be easier than others. Over time, the benefits compound: greater peace, clarity, compassion, and resilience.

> Example: A busy parent began with just two minutes of breath-focused meditation each morning. Over time, they added a gratitude journal and occasional guided meditations. Months later, they found themselves calmer, more present, and more connected to their family and inner life.

Mindfulness and spirituality, though distinct, share a sacred overlap. They invite us to slow down, listen deeply, and live with intention. Whether through prayer, meditation, or a blend of both, these practices offer a path to healing, connection, and peace. In a world that often pulls us outward, they call us gently inward to the still, sacred center of our being.

Journaling for Mental Clarity

Your brain is for thinking, not for storage. When your thoughts are swirling, get them out of your head and onto paper.

In a world overflowing with information, responsibilities, and emotional demands, our minds can quickly become cluttered. We juggle to-do lists, worries, memories, and plans, all while trying to stay present. Journaling offers a simple yet powerful way to clear mental fog, organize thoughts, and reconnect with ourselves.

Why Journaling Works

Our brains are incredible, but they're not designed to store everything. When we try to mentally hold onto every task, worry, and idea, we create cognitive overload. This mental clutter can lead to stress, indecision, and emotional overwhelm.

Journaling acts as a release valve. By putting thoughts on paper (or screen), we externalize what's swirling in our minds. This process frees up mental space, allowing us to think more clearly and calmly.

Beyond decluttering, journaling helps us to see patterns in our thoughts, behaviors, and emotions, organize chaos into coherent narratives, validate feelings by naming and acknowledging them, and create emotional distance, making it easier to respond rather than react.

In short, journaling is not just about writing, it's about witnessing ourselves with compassion and clarity.

The V.O.M.I.T. Method: A Practical Tool for Mental Clarity

One of the most effective journaling techniques for mental clarity is the **V.O.M.I.T. Method**. Despite its humorous name, it's a serious tool for emotional processing and problem-solving. The acronym stands for:

V – Vent

Start by letting it all out. What's bothering you? What's weighing on your heart or mind? Write freely and without censorship. This is your space to be raw, honest, and unfiltered. Don't worry about grammar or structure, just get it out.

O – Obligations

List everything you're carrying: tasks, deadlines, responsibilities, emotional burdens. Seeing it all on paper helps you assess what's truly urgent, what can wait, and what might be delegated or dropped.

M – Mindset

What are you believing about yourself or your situation? Are you telling yourself, "I'm failing," "I'm not enough," or "This will never get better"? Identifying your self-talk helps you challenge unhelpful narratives and shift toward more empowering perspectives.

I – Ideate

Now that you've vented and clarified your mindset, brainstorm possible solutions or shifts. What could help? What's within your control? Don't worry about being perfect—just explore options.

T – Trajectory

End by choosing one small step forward. What's one thing you can do today to move in a better direction? It might be sending an email, taking a walk, asking for help, or simply resting.

Why It Works

The V.O.M.I.T. Method is effective because it moves you from emotional release to actionable clarity. It validates your feelings while encouraging forward motion and takes just 10–15 minutes. It also can be done anywhere: in a notebook, on your phone, or even in a voice memo.

> **Example:** Consider someone going through a stressful job transition. Each Sunday evening, they sit down with their journal and use the V.O.M.I.T. method. They vent about their fears, list their weekly tasks, examine their

mindset ("I'm not good enough"), brainstorm job search strategies, and commit to one action, like updating their resume. Over time, this practice becomes a grounding ritual, helping them stay focused and emotionally balanced.

Other Journaling Practices for Mental Clarity

While the V.O.M.I.T. method is a powerful tool, there are many other journaling styles that support mental clarity. Here are a few worth exploring:

Morning Pages (Julia Cameron, *The Artist's Way*)

This practice involves writing three pages of stream-of-consciousness first thing in the morning. No rules, no editing, just write whatever comes to mind. It's a mental decluttering exercise that clears the slate before the day begins.

Gratitude Journaling

Each day, write down 3–5 things you're grateful for. They can be big (a promotion) or small (a good cup of coffee). This simple habit shifts your focus from problems to blessings and rewires your brain toward positivity.

I am fortunate that my mother kept a gratitude journal for most of her adult life. After she died, my siblings and I began re-reading her entries. I won't share their contents here; they're too personal. But what we discovered was extraordinary: her love of family, her mental clarity, and her hope for humanity shine through every word she wrote. Gratitude was everything to her, especially when she had so little else. Her journals are proof that the practice transforms lives.

Prompt-Based Journaling

Using prompts can help you dive deeper into your thoughts and emotions. Try questions like, "What do I need to let go of today?", "What brought me joy this week?", or "What's one thing I'm proud of?"

These prompts guide your reflection and help you uncover insights you might otherwise miss.

Bullet Journaling for Mental Clarity

You don't need elaborate designs or artistic flair.

A minimalist bullet journal can be a powerful tool for organizing your thoughts. Use it for brain dumps where you write down everything on your mind, priority lists that identify what truly matters today, and delegation lists where you note what can be handed off or postponed. This visual organization helps reduce overwhelm and increase focus.

Conclusion

Journaling is more than a hobby, it's a lifeline for mental clarity. Whether you're navigating stress, seeking insight, or simply trying to stay organized, writing offers a safe space to process, reflect, and plan. With tools like the V.O.M.I.T. method, morning pages, and gratitude journaling, you can create a practice that supports your emotional well-being and helps you move through life with greater clarity and calm.

When Mindfulness isn't Enough

Mindfulness is a powerful tool. It helps us slow down, breathe, and become present with our thoughts and emotions. It can reduce stress, improve focus, and foster emotional resilience.

But it's important to remember mindfulness is a tool, not a cure. It is not a substitute for professional mental health care. Sometimes you need the entire toolbox, and that's okay.

When to Seek Additional Support

Consider reaching out to a mental health professional if you experience:

- Persistent anxiety or depression that doesn't improve with mindfulness

- Intrusive thoughts that feel overwhelming or unmanageable

- Symptoms of trauma, such as flashbacks, hypervigilance, or emotional numbness

- Increased distress during mindfulness practice (sometimes sitting with emotions can be triggering)

There is no shame in seeking help. In fact, recognizing when you need more support is a sign of strength and self-awareness.

Mindfulness + Therapy = A Powerful Combination

Many therapists integrate mindfulness into evidence-based treatments such as DBT (Dialectical Behavior Therapy), which combines mindfulness with emotional regulation and interpersonal skills; ACT (Acceptance and Commitment Therapy), which uses mindfulness to help people accept difficult emotions and commit to values-based action; and MBSR (Mindfulness-Based Stress Reduction), a structured program that blends mindfulness with stress management techniques.

Therapy provides tools that mindfulness alone cannot, like coping strategies, emotional processing, and personalized guidance. Together, mindfulness and therapy can create a holistic path to healing and growth.

Bringing it all Together

Mindfulness isn't about perfection, it's about presence.

It's not a performance, and it's not reserved for monks or mystics. It's simply the practice of showing up for your life, one moment at a time. You don't need hours of silence or a mountaintop retreat. You just need moments... moments to breathe, to notice, to pause.

Whether you choose breath work, prayer, meditation, or journaling, you're doing something profound: you're creating space. Space between stimulus and response. Space between thought and action. Space to feel, to reflect, to reset.

And in that space, clarity lives.

Clarity doesn't mean having all the answers. It means seeing more clearly what's true for you, what hurts, what heals. It's the beginning of wisdom, and it starts with a single breath.

The Invitation

Start with one practice.

Try it for a week.

You don't have to change your whole life overnight. Just notice what shifts—not necessarily in your circumstances, but in how you relate to them. That's where transformation begins.

Permission to Be Human

If your mind wanders, that's okay. If you forget a day, that's okay. If you feel overwhelmed, that's okay.

You're not failing. You're practicing.

And remember: You don't have to quiet the storm. You just have to quiet your mind enough to hear your own wisdom.

You should sit in meditation for twenty minutes every day—unless you're too busy. Then you should sit for an hour. (Zen proverb)

Reflection Prompt

Reflection Questions

- When do I feel most present? When do I feel most scattered?
- What thoughts or worries take up the most space in my mind?
- What would it feel like to observe my thoughts without believing all of them?
- Which mindfulness practice feels most natural to me right now?
- What's one moment today I can be fully present for?
- If I gave myself 5 minutes of stillness each day, what might change?

Instruction: Choose one question and journal on it. Don't overthink, just write what comes.

Instructions: Choose ONE practice to try each day this week. Notice what you learn.

Day 1: Breath Awareness

- Spend 3 minutes focusing only on your breath
- Count 10 breaths, then start over
- Notice: Did your mind wander? How many times? (That's normal!)

Day 2: 5-4-3-2-1 Grounding

- Use this when you feel stressed or anxious
- Go through all five senses slowly
- Notice: Did it help you feel more present?

Day 3: Mindful Moments

- Pick one daily activity (eating, walking, showering)
- Do it with full attention—no phone, no multitasking
- Notice: What did you observe that you usually miss?

Day 4: Body Scan

- Before bed, scan your body from head to toe

- Notice where you hold tension

- Notice: Does this help you sleep better?

Day 5: Thought Observation

- Sit for 5 minutes and watch your thoughts

- Label them: "worrying," "planning," "remembering"

- Notice: Can you see thoughts as passing events, not facts?

Day 6: Prayer or Meditation

- Try one contemplative practice (centering prayer, loving-kindness, mantra)

- Even 3 minutes counts

- Notice: How does this feel different from other practices?

Day 7: Journaling (V.O.M.I.T. Method)

- Write through all five steps

- Notice: Did getting it on paper create clarity?

End-of-week reflection:

- Which practice felt most helpful?

- Which was hardest?

- What will you continue?

Quick Reference: Practices at a Glance

When you need...	Try this practice
Immediate calm	Box Breathing (4-4-4-4)
To stop spiraling	5-4-3-2-1 Grounding
To release tension	Body Scan
To process emotions	V.O.M.I.T. Journaling
To connect spiritually	Prayer or Meditation
To build daily habit	Mindful Moments
To observe thoughts	Thought Observation

Healthy Habits for a Healthy Mind

---

*Take care of your body. It's the only place
you have to live. (Rohn)*

We often talk about mental health as if it lives in a vacuum—and something that happens only in our thoughts, emotions, or behaviors. But the truth is, mental health lives in a body. Your brain isn't floating in space, detached from the rest of you. It's an organ, just like your heart or lungs, and it's deeply affected by how you treat your body.

Think about it: what you eat, how you move, and how you sleep all shape your mood, your energy, and your ability to cope with stress. The connection between mind and body isn't just poetic, it's biological. Hormones, neurotransmitters, blood sugar levels, inflammation, and even gut health all play a role in how you feel mentally and emotionally.

Imagine someone who's been feeling anxious, foggy, and emotionally drained. They start to wonder if they're having a mental health crisis. But when they pause and take inventory, they realize they've been running on caffeine, skipping meals, getting five hours of sleep a night, and not moving their body in days. No wonder they feel off. When they begin to address the basics--eating nourishing food, getting some movement, and prioritizing sleep— their mood stabilizes, their thoughts become clearer, and their anxiety softens. What felt like a crisis was, in part, a body crying out for care.

This isn't to say that all mental health struggles can be solved with a smoothie and a walk. But it is to say that mental health and physical health are inseparable. And yet, we often treat them as two different worlds.

Modern medicine tends to compartmentalize: you see a therapist for your mind, a doctor for your body. But ancient wisdom knew better. The Latin phrase *mens sana in corpore sano*, "a healthy mind in a healthy body", wasn't just a slogan. It was a recognition that the two are deeply intertwined. You can't think your way out of exhaustion. You can't meditate your way out of chronic sleep deprivation. And you certainly can't journal your way out of malnutrition.

Your brain needs fuel, movement, and rest. It needs the same care and attention you'd give to any other part of your body. When we ignore this connection, we risk missing a foundational piece of mental wellness.

That's what this chapter is about: building a foundation, not perfection or rigid routines, but small, sustainable habits that nourish both body and mind.

We'll explore three essential pillars: Nourishment, Movement, and Sleep. These aren't just lifestyle choices, they're mental health tools. And we'll also look at how to use technology wisely, not as a tyrant that steals your attention, but as a tool that can support your habits and help you stay on track.

The Trifecta – Nourishment, Movement, Sleep

When it comes to supporting mental health, it's easy to get distracted by trendy supplements, complex wellness routines, or the latest biohacks. But the truth is, the most powerful tools for a healthy mind are often the simplest—and they're already within your reach. Nourishment, movement, and sleep form the trifecta of foundational habits that directly shape your emotional resilience, mental clarity, and overall well-being.

These three aren't just helpful, they're essential. Your brain needs fuel from nutritious food, stimulation from physical activity, and restoration from quality sleep. When even one of these is neglected, the others tend to suffer. You might notice it in subtle ways: poor sleep leads to sugar cravings, which lead to skipped workouts, which lead to even worse sleep. It's a vicious cycle that can leave you feeling foggy, anxious, and emotionally drained.

But the good news? The cycle works in the other direction too. A good night's sleep helps you make better food choices. Nourishing meals give you energy to move your body. Movement helps you sleep more deeply. It's a virtuous (and at times vicious) cycle, and once you get it going, even in small ways, it builds momentum.

That's why this chapter focuses on these three pillars. Not because you need to become a fitness guru or follow a perfect routine, but because small, consistent improvements in these areas can lead to outsized benefits. This is the 80/20 principle in action: you don't need to do everything perfectly. You just need to do the basics well, most of the time.

This chapter isn't about adding stress to your life, it's about removing obstacles to your well-being. It's about helping you feel more grounded, more energized, and more mentally clear. And it's about using technology wisely not as a distraction, but as a support system for your habits.

So, let's begin with the basics. Because when you care for your body, you're also caring for your mind and that's where real change begins.

Nourishment – Food as Fuel and Medicine

Let's start with what you put into your body. Food isn't just fuel, it's information. Every bite you take sends signals to your cells, including the ones in your brain. It influences how you feel, how you think, and how well you cope with stress. And while we often talk about nutrition in terms of weight or fitness, its impact on mental health is just as profound—if not more so.

I used the word "nourishment" intentionally. It is a term that we use at home to place more of an emphasis on what food does for us and less on "eating dinner because it's 6:00." So, don't be alarmed if you are ever at our house and you hear, "Do you want to take some nourishment?"

The Brain-Food Connection

Your brain is a high-maintenance organ. Though it only makes up about 2% of your body weight, it consumes roughly 20% of your energy. That means it's constantly demanding a steady supply of glucose, healthy fats, amino acids, vitamins, and minerals to function properly. When those needs aren't met, the first thing to suffer is often mental clarity.

Think about the last time you skipped a meal or lived off vending machine snacks for a day. Did you feel foggy, irritable, or anxious? That's not just coincidence; it's chemistry. Blood sugar swings can lead to mood instability, while deficiencies in key nutrients like B vitamins, magnesium, and omega-3 fatty acids are linked to depression, fatigue, and even cognitive decline. One of our sons is notorious for getting "hangry". The moment his blood sugar drops, so does his mood: irritable, short-tempered, unreasonable. A simple snack transforms him back into himself. It's a clear reminder that brain chemistry isn't abstract, it's real, immediate, and powerful.

And then there's the gut-brain axis: a fascinating and increasingly studied connection between your digestive system and your emotional state. About 90% of your serotonin, the feel-good neurotransmitter, is produced in the gut. This gut-brain connection explains why digestive issues often accompany anxiety and depression, and why those 'butterflies' in your stomach before a presentation are more than a metaphor. Your gut and brain are in constant communication, which is why gut health is mental health.

Unfortunately, the typical Western diet doesn't do our brains any favors. It's dominated by ultra-processed foods, high in sugar, trans fats, and artificial additives, and low in the nutrients our brains crave. These foods are engineered to be addictive, not nourishing. They're convenient, yes, but they come at a cost: increased inflammation, unstable energy, and a higher risk of anxiety and depression.

Principles of Nourishing Your Mind

So, what does it look like to eat for mental clarity and emotional resilience? It's not about restriction or perfection; it's about supporting your brain with what it needs to thrive.

Start with whole foods. Fruits, vegetables, whole grains, lean proteins, and healthy fats are the building blocks of a brain-friendly diet. These are foods your great-grandmother would recognize: simple, real, and nutrient-dense. Instead of obsessing over what to cut out, focus on what to add in. One person I worked with started adding a smoothie to their morning routine: just spinach, berries, banana, and a scoop of protein. Within a week, they noticed better focus and more stable energy throughout the day.

Speaking of protein, it's essential for mental health. Proteins break down into amino acids, which your brain uses to make neurotransmitters like serotonin and dopamine. Including protein at every meal, especially breakfast, can help stabilize blood sugar and reduce mood swings. Think eggs, Greek yogurt, beans, fish, chicken, tofu, or nuts.

Then there are healthy fats, which your brain absolutely loves. In fact, your brain is about 60% fat, and it needs quality fats to function well. Omega-3 fatty acids, found in salmon, walnuts, flaxseed, and chia seeds, are especially important. They've been linked to reduced symptoms of depression and improved cognitive function. On the flip side, trans fats and excessive omega-6s (common in processed snacks and fried foods) can increase inflammation and worsen mood.

Of course, sugar and processed foods are worth limiting, not eliminating entirely, but keeping in check. Sugar spikes lead to crashes, which lead to cravings, which can trigger anxiety and fatigue. It's not about never having dessert; it's about not making dessert your foundation. For those of us with diabetes, glucose intake becomes even more of a serious consideration.

And don't forget hydration. Your brain is about 75% water, and even mild dehydration can affect mood, concentration, and energy. My wife drinks water like it were the Eleventh Commandment. Aim to make water your primary beverage, and be mindful of excess caffeine and alcohol, which can disrupt sleep and mood regulation.

One more simple but powerful habit: don't skip meals. Your brain needs consistent fuel. Skipping meals can lead to low blood sugar, irritability, poor focus, and decision fatigue. Regular eating helps stabilize your mood and energy throughout the day.

Practical Strategies for Real Life

Eating well doesn't have to be complicated. One of the most effective strategies is meal prep for mental health. Spend a little time on Sunday chopping vegetables, cooking grains, boiling eggs, or making a batch of soup. Having healthy options ready to go during the week removes decision fatigue and makes it easier to nourish yourself even on busy days.

Think in terms of the 80/20 approach: aim for 80% whole, nourishing foods, and leave 20% for flexibility, treats, social meals, and joy. Perfection isn't the goal. Consistency is.

And as we discussed in the previous chapter, mindful eating can transform your relationship with food. Slow down. Taste your food. Notice when you're hungry and when you're full. This not only reduces overeating but also improves digestion and helps you tune into your body's needs.

Sometimes, even with a solid diet, people benefit from supplements—especially if they have specific deficiencies. Common ones that support mental health include Vitamin D, B-complex, and Omega-3s. But it's important to consult a healthcare provider before starting anything new. Don't rely on internet trends or self-diagnosis.

I've seen firsthand how small changes can make a big difference. One friend used to skip breakfast entirely, relying on coffee until lunch. She often felt anxious and scattered by mid-morning. When she started eating a simple breakfast, eggs and toast, or oatmeal with nuts, her energy stabilized, and her mood improved dramatically. It wasn't a miracle cure, but it was a meaningful shift.

What NOT to Do

As you begin to nourish your mind through food, it's just as important to avoid common pitfalls.

First, extreme dieting or restriction can backfire. It might promise quick results, but it often leads to anxiety, obsessive thoughts, and nutrient deficiencies. Your brain needs adequate calories and variety to function well.

Second, be mindful of using food as your primary emotional coping tool. It's okay to find comfort in food as many of us do. But if food becomes your only way to soothe stress or sadness, it may be time to explore other coping strategies, like journaling, movement, or talking to someone.

And finally, avoid moralizing food—labeling things as "good" or "bad." This creates guilt and shame around eating, which can damage your relationship with food and your body. All foods can fit into a balanced approach. Nourishment is about adding health, not subtracting joy.

A note for parents: Avoid using food as reward or punishment. When we say, 'Finish your vegetables and you can have dessert' or 'No snack because you misbehaved,' we teach children to associate nourishment with external factors rather than internal hunger cues. Food is nourishment, not currency.

Let food be thy medicine and medicine be thy food. (Hippocrates)

Movement – Exercise for Mental Clarity

Your body was designed to move. And when you do, your mind benefits profoundly. Here's the truth: if you stop moving, eventually you won't be able to move.

We often think of exercise as something we do for physical health, weight management, cardiovascular fitness, strength. But movement is just as essential for mental health. In fact, the science is clear: regular physical activity is one of the most effective tools we have for improving mood, reducing anxiety, and enhancing mental clarity.

Exercise has been shown to be as effective as medication for mild to moderate depression. It releases endorphins, your body's natural mood elevators, and increases BDNF (brain-derived neurotrophic factor), a kind of fertilizer for your brain that helps grow new cells and strengthen neural connections. Movement also improves sleep, boosts self-esteem, and enhances cognitive function, including memory and focus.

But the benefits go beyond biology. Movement gives you a sense of agency, a reminder that you can do something, even when life feels overwhelming. It provides structure and routine, which are stabilizing forces for mental health. It can offer social connection when done with others, or solitude and reflection when done alone. And perhaps most importantly, it creates space: a break from screens, stressors, and the constant noise of daily life.

You don't have to love exercise. You don't have to become an athlete. You just have to move, regularly, intentionally, and with compassion for your body.

Types of Movement and Their Benefits

There's no one-size-fits-all approach to movement. What matters is finding something you'll actually do, and ideally, something you'll enjoy (or at least not dread).

Aerobic exercise, also known as cardio, is especially powerful for mental health. Activities like walking, running, cycling, swimming, and dancing increase heart rate and circulation, which helps regulate mood and reduce symptoms of anxiety and depression. Research suggests that 20–30 minutes most days is ideal, but even 10 minutes can make a difference.

For some people, movement becomes a core part of their identity and mental wellness routine. Whether it's training for marathons or simply jogging around the neighborhood, the consistency and rhythm of running can be deeply grounding. It's not just about fitness, it's about feeling alive, capable, and connected to something bigger than yourself.

Strength training, using weights, resistance bands, or bodyweight exercises, also offers significant mental health benefits. It builds confidence, improves body image, and helps with sleep quality. You don't need a gym membership or fancy equipment. Two to three sessions per week, even at home, can be enough to feel stronger and more mentally resilient.

Yoga and stretching combine movement with breath and mindfulness. These practices reduce cortisol, the stress hormone, and improve flexibility, body awareness, and emotional regulation. Yoga is accessible to all fitness levels and can be adapted to suit your needs whether you want a gentle flow or a more intense practice.

And then there's walking—the underrated champion of mental health. It's free, accessible, and low-impact. Walking outdoors adds an extra layer of benefit, thanks to the calming effects of nature. It can be social (a walk with a friend) or meditative (a solo stroll with your thoughts).

You know by now that my wife is a runner. We like to kid her by saying that we like her much better when she runs. After a run, there is a dramatic shift in her mood and anxiety levels. For her, it is so much more than burning calories or exercise, it is about creating mental space to be herself.

Overcoming Barriers to Movement

Of course, knowing movement is good for you doesn't always make it easy to do. Life gets busy. Energy runs low. Motivation fades. But most barriers to movement can be overcome with small shifts in mindset and strategy.

One common obstacle is "I don't have time." But here's the truth: 10 minutes counts. You can break it up: 10 minutes in the morning, 10 minutes in the evening. Walk during your lunch break. Take the stairs. Park farther away. Movement doesn't have to be a big production.

Another is "I'm too tired." It's a paradox, but movement actually increases energy. Start small, just five minutes. Often, once you begin, momentum builds. Movement is often the cure for fatigue, not the cause.

"I hate gyms." That's fine, you don't need one. Walk outside. Do bodyweight exercises at home. Dance in your living room. YouTube is full of free workout videos for every level and interest.

"I'm not athletic." Movement is for everyone, not just athletes. Start where you are. Walk around the block. Do five squats. Stretch for five minutes. Every journey begins with one step.

"I'm too out of shape." That's exactly why you should start. You don't have to be good at it; you just have to do it. Your body will adapt. Your mind will thank you.

The key is to find what you'll actually do. Don't force yourself into activities you hate. Try different things until something clicks. Enjoyment, or at least tolerance, is essential for consistency.

Practical Strategies for Building a Movement Habit

Creating a sustainable movement habit doesn't require willpower, it requires strategy.

Start stupidly small. Five minutes is better than zero minutes. Commit to putting on your shoes and stepping outside. Often, that's all it takes to get going.

Tie movement to existing habits. After your morning coffee, walk for 10 minutes. Before dinner, do 10 push-ups. Habit stacking makes it easier to remember and follow through.

Make it social or solitary, whatever you need. Some people thrive with accountability. Join a class, find a workout buddy, or schedule regular walks with a friend. Others need alone time. A solo walk or home workout can be just as powerful.

Track your progress but don't obsess. Notice how you feel after movement. Track consistency, not perfection. Celebrate showing up, regardless of intensity. The goal isn't to hit a number, it's to build a habit that supports your mental health.

Movement is medicine. It's not about sculpting your body, it's about supporting your mind. Whether it's a walk, a stretch, a dance, or a run, every bit of movement is a step toward clarity, resilience, and emotional balance.

Sleep – The Foundation of Everything

If nourishment and movement are the pillars of mental health, sleep is the foundation. Without it, everything crumbles.

You can eat well and exercise daily, but if you're not sleeping, your brain and body will struggle. Sleep isn't just rest, it's restoration. It's when your brain processes emotions, consolidates memories, clears out waste, and resets your stress response. It's when your body repairs itself, balances hormones, and prepares you to face another day.

Sleep is your superpower. During deep sleep, your brain literally detoxifies itself, flushing out metabolic waste that builds up during waking hours. REM sleep, the stage where dreams occur, helps you process emotions and integrate experiences. Sleep also regulates your mood, sharpens your decision-making, and strengthens your immune system.

When you don't sleep, everything suffers. Anxiety and depression increase. Irritability spikes. Judgment and impulse control decline. Your physical health takes a hit: your immune system weakens, your risk of heart disease rises, and your metabolism slows. After just 24 hours without sleep, your cognitive function drops to the level of someone who's legally intoxicated (Williamson & Feyer, 2000).

And here's the tricky part: poor mental health makes it harder to sleep, and poor sleep worsens mental health. It's a vicious cycle. Breaking that loop is one of the most powerful things you can do for your well-being.

So how much sleep do you actually need? For most adults, the sweet spot is 7 to 9 hours per night. Not five or six hours during the week with a weekend "catch-up", that doesn't work. Sleep debt accumulates, and you can't fully repay it with a few extra hours on Saturday. And it's not just about quantity. Quality matters just as much. Deep, uninterrupted sleep is what your brain craves.

Common Sleep Disruptors

If sleep is so essential, why do so many of us struggle with it? The answer often lies in our habits and environments.

One major culprit is screen time before bed. The blue light emitted by phones, tablets, and TVs suppresses melatonin, the hormone that signals your body it's time to sleep. And it's not just the light, it's the content. News, social media, and work emails activate your stress response. Your brain doesn't distinguish between digital drama and real-life danger.

Another disruptor is an inconsistent sleep schedule. Going to bed and waking up at different times confuses your circadian rhythm, the internal clock that regulates sleep. Weekend "catch-up sleep" might feel good in the moment, but it doesn't reset the deficit. Your body thrives on routine. For me, setting a bedtime alarm is more important than setting a wake-up alarm. Try it for a week or so.

Caffeine and alcohol also play a role. Caffeine has a half-life of about six hours, which means that afternoon coffee can still be in your system at bedtime. Alcohol might help you fall asleep, but it disrupts sleep quality, especially REM sleep, the stage where dreams occur, which is crucial for emotional processing.

Then there's stress and racing thoughts. You lie down, and suddenly your mind starts replaying the day, worrying about tomorrow, or spiraling into "what ifs." This is where mindfulness practices from earlier chapters, like breathwork, body scans, and journaling, can help quiet the mental noise.

Finally, your sleep environment matters more than you might think. A room that's too hot, too bright, or too noisy can sabotage your sleep. So can an uncomfortable mattress or using your bedroom as a workspace. If your brain associates your bed with emails and deadlines, it won't associate it with rest.

During the COVID-19 pandemic, many people suddenly had to work and learn from home. Dining tables became classrooms, bedrooms became conference rooms, and the boundaries between work and rest blurred. This made it even harder to sleep; Our brains couldn't distinguish between workspace and rest space. If you're still working from home, consider whether your bedroom has become too associated with work. If so, reclaim it as a sanctuary for rest.

Building a Sleep Routine That Works

The good news is that sleep can be trained. Just like any habit, it responds to consistency and cues. Creating a wind-down ritual, a set of calming activities before bed, can signal to your brain that it's time to shift gears.

Start by dimming the lights. Bright overhead lighting tells your brain it's still daytime. Switch to lamps, then candlelight if you like. This gradual dimming helps your body start producing melatonin naturally.

Next, turn off screens at least 30 minutes before bed, ideally 60. If you must use your phone, switch to night mode or use a blue light filter. Better yet, pick up a physical book. Reading something gentle and non-stimulating can ease the transition to sleep.

Do something calming. Gentle yoga or stretching, journaling (especially using the V.O.M.I.T. method to clear your mind), prayer, meditation, or a warm bath can all help. Interestingly, the drop in body temperature after a bath or shower helps signal sleep readiness.

The key is consistency. It doesn't matter exactly what you do, what matters is doing it regularly. Your brain learns routines. When you repeat the same wind-down activities each night, it starts to associate them with sleep.

One person I worked with struggled with insomnia for years. She started a simple wind-down routine: phone off at 9 p.m., herbal tea, 10 minutes of journaling, and 20 minutes of reading. Within two weeks, her sleep improved dramatically, not because she found a magic cure, but because she created a consistent, calming rhythm.

You can also optimize your sleep environment. Aim for a room that's cool, dark, and quiet. The ideal temperature is between 60–67°F. Use blackout curtains or a sleep mask to block light. If noise is an issue, try a white noise machine or earplugs.

Reserve your bed for sleep (and sex): not work, scrolling, or watching TV. Train your brain to associate your bed with rest. And invest in comfortable bedding. A quality mattress, supportive pillows, and clean, high-quality sheets can make a surprisingly big difference.

Here's our setup, and I have to admit we'd both win gold medals at the Sleep Olympics. We keep it cool at 65°F with room-darkening shades and a box fan for white noise. We use 1200-count sheets washed weekly (any less is like sleeping on hay!) and quality pillows. My wife recently added an eye mask—apparently her definition of 'pitch black' differs from my 'dark.' She also uses earplugs with a selection of white noises. Somehow, this works for us!"

If Sleep Won't Come

Sometimes, even with the best routine, sleep doesn't arrive. That's when the 20-minute rule comes in handy. If you're lying in bed and still awake after 20 minutes, get up. Do something boring in low light such as reading a dull book, stretching gently, or sitting quietly. Return to bed when you feel sleepy. Lying awake and stressing about not sleeping only makes it harder.

You can also revisit practices from Chapter 6. A body scan meditation, breath awareness, or progressive muscle relaxation can help calm your nervous system and prepare your body for rest. Try the 4-7-8 breathing technique: inhale for 4 seconds, hold for 7, exhale for 8. It's simple, soothing, and effective.

If sleep problems persist, it may be time to seek help. Chronic insomnia, trouble sleeping three or more nights a week for three months or longer, can benefit from professional support. So can sleep apnea (often marked by snoring, gasping, or daytime exhaustion), restless leg syndrome, or other sleep disorders. A sleep specialist or CBT-I therapist (cognitive behavioral therapy for insomnia) can be life-changing.

The Power of Naps (Optional Bonus)

While nighttime sleep is the priority, strategic napping can be a helpful supplement. A 20-minute power nap can boost alertness and mood without causing grogginess. The best time to nap is early afternoon, between 1 and 3 p.m. Longer naps (over 30 minutes) risk sleep inertia, that heavy, disoriented feeling upon waking.

Naps aren't a substitute for a good night's sleep, but they can be a useful tool especially on days when rest was interrupted or stress is high.

Sleep isn't a luxury; it's a biological necessity. It's the foundation of mental clarity, emotional resilience, and physical health. When you prioritize sleep, you're not being lazy, you're being wise. You're giving your brain the restoration it needs to show up fully for life.

Sleep is the best meditation. (Dalai Lama)

Technology as Tool, Not Tyrant

We've talked about boundaries with technology back in Chapter 5, how constant notifications, endless scrolling, and digital overload can hijack your attention and drain your energy. Now, let's shift the lens and explore how technology, when used intentionally, can actually support your health habits. Because like most tools, it's not inherently good or bad—it depends on how you use it.

The Double-Edged Sword

Technology is a double-edged sword when it comes to mental health.

On one side, it can harm. Doomscrolling through bad news, comparing yourself to filtered lives on social media, staying up late glued to screens, and sitting for hours without moving all can erode your mental clarity and emotional resilience.

But on the other side, technology can help. It can track your movement, remind you to drink water, guide you through a meditation, connect you to supportive communities, and hold you accountable to your goals. It can educate, motivate, and even inspire.

The key is intentional use. Technology should serve you, not the other way around. Set it up to support your goals, then step back. Use it as a guide, not a master. And if tracking starts to feel obsessive or stressful, it's okay to pause or stop. Your mental health comes first.

Fitness Tracking: Move More, Stress Less

One of the simplest ways to use technology for mental health is to track your movement. Most smartphones have built-in step counters, and wearables like Fitbit, Apple Watch, Garmin, or Oura Ring can give you even more data.

A good goal for most people is 7,000 to 10,000 steps per day. You don't need to obsess over hitting 10,000. Research shows that even 7,000 steps can significantly improve health outcomes. The real benefit is the visual reminder to move. Seeing your step count can nudge you to take the stairs, walk during lunch, or stretch between meetings.

Apps like Strava (for running and cycling), Strong (for weightlifting), and Peloton (for guided classes) can help you log workouts and track progress. Free options like Nike Training Club or YouTube workout channels offer accessible routines for all fitness levels.

Some wearables also track heart rate and recovery metrics like HRV (heart rate variability), which can give insight into your nervous system and stress levels. These features are more advanced, but useful if you're interested in deeper data.

Just remember: don't let the numbers become a source of anxiety. Rest days are part of the data too. If tracking starts to feel like pressure instead of support, it's okay to take a break.

One person I know realized they were sitting for over 10 hours a day. They set hourly movement reminders on their smartwatch; just a nudge to stand up, stretch, or walk around. Within a week, they felt more energized, less stiff, and surprisingly more focused.

Nutrition Tracking: Awareness Without Obsession

Tracking what you eat can be helpful if done with care. Apps like MyFitnessPal, Cronometer, and Lose It allow you to log meals and see patterns. You might notice you're consistently low on protein, skipping vegetables, or relying on sugar for energy. This awareness can lead to small, meaningful changes.

Hydration tracking is even simpler. Some apps send reminders to drink water, but honestly, just carrying a water bottle and refilling it a few times a day works just as well.

The goal isn't perfection, it's awareness. Tracking can help you identify nutrient gaps, understand emotional eating patterns, and make more intentional choices. But it's not for everyone.

For some, calorie counting can trigger disordered eating or anxiety. If tracking feels obsessive or stressful, stop. Focus on quality and variety, not just quantity.

A great alternative is the plate method: fill half your plate with vegetables, a quarter with protein, and a quarter with whole grains. No app needed, just a visual guideline that supports balanced eating.

One person tracked their food for two weeks and realized they were eating almost no protein at breakfast. They started adding eggs, Greek yogurt, or nut butter to their morning routine and noticed more stable energy and fewer mid-morning crashes.

Sleep Tracking: Insight Into Your Rest

Sleep tracking can offer valuable insights especially if you're trying to improve your sleep habits. Wearables like Apple Watch, Fitbit, Oura Ring, and Whoop track sleep duration and quality. Apps like Sleep Cycle use your phone's microphone and motion sensors to estimate sleep stages.

These tools can show you patterns: how late nights affect your mood, how alcohol disrupts deep sleep, or how consistent bedtimes improve overall rest. They can motivate you to go to bed earlier or create a better wind-down routine.

But again, don't let the data stress you out. Sleep trackers aren't perfect. They estimate, not measure precisely. And some people actually sleep worse knowing they're being tracked.

If you prefer a low-tech option, try a sleep journal. Each morning, jot down your bedtime, wake time, and how you feel. Over time, you'll see patterns emerge without needing a device.

My wife discovered through her sleep tracker that even one glass of wine before bed consistently disrupted her deep sleep. When she stopped drinking in the evening, her sleep quality improved dramatically and she woke feeling more rested.

Putting Technology in Its Place

Technology is a tool. Use it intentionally, or it will use you.

Here are a few simple guidelines to keep tech in its proper place:

Set it and forget it. Use tracking for a few weeks to gather data. Identify patterns. Make changes. Then let it go. You don't need to track forever.

Turn off most notifications. Choose 2–3 meaningful alerts, like a water reminder or bedtime nudge. Turn off the rest. Your attention is precious.

Use "Do Not Disturb" modes. During meals, family time, or your wind-down routine, silence the noise. Your health matters more than instant replies.

Take technology fasts. One day a week, skip the tracking. Notice how you feel. If you feel relief, consider scaling back. Your body knows what it needs, sometimes better than your devices do.

Technology can be a powerful ally in your journey toward mental clarity and emotional resilience. But only if you're in charge. Use it to support your habits, not control them. Let it guide you, not guilt you. And remember: you are the expert on your own well-being—not your watch, not your app, not your step count.

Building Sustainable Habits

Knowledge is useless without action. You can read every book, listen to every podcast, and understand every principle—but if it doesn't translate into your daily life, it won't change much. So, let's talk about how to actually build these habits into your routine in a way that feels doable, not overwhelming.

The truth is that most people don't struggle because they don't know what to do. They struggle because they try to do too much, too fast, and burn out. The key to lasting change isn't intensity it's consistency. And that starts with small steps.

The 1% Improvement Philosophy

Imagine improving by just 1% each day. It doesn't sound like much, but over time, it adds up to 37 times better in a year, thanks to the power of compounding. This idea, popularized by James Clear in *Atomic Habits*, is simple but profound: small daily improvements lead to massive long-term results.

You don't need to overhaul your life overnight. You don't need to become a wellness expert or follow a rigid routine. You just need to aim for what is sustainable, not perfect.

Clear shares the story of the British cycling team, which went from mediocre to dominant by improving just 1% in every area: nutrition, training, sleep, equipment. No single change was revolutionary, but together, they transformed the team's performance. That's the power of small, intentional shifts.

Start With One

When it comes to building habits, less is more. Don't try to fix everything at once. Pick one habit to focus on for the next 2–4 weeks. Once it feels automatic, like brushing your teeth, add the next one. This approach prevents you from becoming overwhelmed and gives each habit the attention it needs to stick.

Here's what a simple progression might look like:

Week 1–2: Drink a glass of water first thing every morning.

Week 3–4: Add a 10-minute morning walk.

Week 5–6: Establish a consistent bedtime.

Week 7–8: Add protein to your breakfast.

Each habit builds on the last, creating a foundation of wellness that feels natural, not forced. And because you're not rushing, you're more likely to keep going.

The Power of Habit Stacking

One of the easiest ways to build new habits is to tie them to existing ones, a strategy known as habit stacking. You're already doing dozens of things every day without thinking: brushing your teeth, pouring coffee, eating dinner, getting into bed. These routines can become anchors for new behaviors.

For example:

> After I brush my teeth, I do 10 push-ups.
>
> After I pour my coffee, I drink a glass of water.
>
> After I eat dinner, I take a 10-minute walk.
>
> After I get into bed, I do a 5-minute body scan.

This works because your brain already recognizes the first habit as part of your routine. By attaching a new habit to it, you reduce decision fatigue and increase the likelihood of follow-through. Over time, these stacked habits become seamless parts of your day.

Building sustainable habits isn't about willpower, it's about strategy. Start small. Be consistent. Stack habits. And most importantly, be kind to yourself. Progress isn't linear, and perfection isn't the goal. What matters is showing up, day after day, and trusting that small steps lead to big change.

Closing: The Foundation of Resilience

We've covered a lot, nourishment, movement, sleep, and the role of technology. And now, it's time to bring it all together.

These habits aren't luxuries. They're necessities. Your mental health doesn't float above your body as much as it lives in it. Every thought, emotion, and decision is shaped by how well your body is cared for. When you nourish yourself, move regularly, and sleep deeply, you're not just improving your physical health, you're also building the foundation of resilience.

This isn't about chasing perfection. It's about showing up for yourself in small, consistent ways. Because those small actions compound. Better sleep gives you more energy to move.

Movement improves your mood and appetite. Nourishing food helps you sleep better. It's a virtuous cycle, and each pillar supports the others.

And yes, some days you'll eat pizza and skip the gym. Some nights you'll stay up too late. Some mornings you'll forget to drink water. That's okay. You don't have to be perfect. Rest days are part of the plan. What matters is that you keep coming back. Consistency over perfection, always.

So, as you move forward, remember this:

"Your body is not a machine. It's your home. Treat it with respect, nourish it with intention, and move it with gratitude."

You've laid the groundwork. You've built a foundation. But we don't exist in isolation. Our well-being is deeply connected to others—through relationships, community, and shared experience.

Let's now explore the power of human connection.

Reflection Prompt

Reflection Questions:

- Which of the three pillars (nourishment, movement, sleep) needs the most attention right now?
- What's one small change I could make this week in each area?
- What barriers am I using as excuses? Are they real or stories I'm telling myself?
- How do I feel when I prioritize these habits vs. when I neglect them?
- What would my life look like if I made these habits non-negotiable?
- Who can support me in building healthier habits?

Instruction: Choose one question and write honestly. Notice what comes up without judgment.

Healthy Habits Tracker

Instructions: Use this tracker for one week to build awareness. Check off each habit as you complete it. Notice patterns without judgment.

Weekly Tracker

HABIT	M	T	W	T	F	S	S
NOURISHMENT							
Ate breakfast with protein	☐	☐	☐	☐	☐	☐	☐
Ate 3+ servings vegetables	☐	☐	☐	☐	☐	☐	☐
Drank 6-8 glasses water	☐	☐	☐	☐	☐	☐	☐
Limited sugar/processed foods	☐	☐	☐	☐	☐	☐	☐
MOVEMENT							
20+ min intentional movement	☐	☐	☐	☐	☐	☐	☐
Took the stairs/parked far	☐	☐	☐	☐	☐	☐	☐
Stretched or did yoga	☐	☐	☐	☐	☐	☐	☐
SLEEP							
In bed by [YOUR TIME]	☐	☐	☐	☐	☐	☐	☐
7-9 hours of sleep	☐	☐	☐	☐	☐	☐	☐
No screens 30 min before bed	☐	☐	☐	☐	☐	☐	☐
Wind-down routine	☐	☐	☐	☐	☐	☐	☐

Weekly Reflection:

Which habit was easiest to maintain?

Which was most challenging?

What patterns did I notice?

How did I feel on days when I hit most/all habits?

What's one habit I'll prioritize next week?

Notes:

Alternative: Simple Daily Check-In

For those who don't want to track specific habits, offer a simpler version:

Each evening, answer these three questions:

1. Did I nourish my body today? (Yes / Mostly / Needs work)

2. Did I move my body today? (Yes / Mostly / Needs work)

3. Did I prioritize sleep last night? (Yes / Mostly / Needs work)

Notice trends over a week without obsessing over details.

Small daily improvements are the key to staggering long-term results. (Clear)

Strength in Connection

The Isolation Epidemic

We live in a time of unprecedented digital connection. We can message someone across the world in seconds, join video calls from our living rooms, and scroll through hundreds of updates from friends, acquaintances, and strangers. And yet, loneliness is at an all-time high.

It's a strange paradox. We're surrounded by people, online, at work, in our neighborhoods, but many of us feel deeply alone. We're drowning in shallow connections while starving for deep ones. Consider someone with 500 Facebook friends, dozens of Instagram followers, and a buzzing group chat, yet no one they feel safe calling at 2 AM when they're struggling. That's not connection. That's proximity without intimacy.

The Paradox of Modern Connection

Modern life has blurred the lines between visibility and connection. We mistake being seen for being known. We confuse being busy with being bonded. We scroll through curated glimpses of other people's lives instead of sharing our own in meaningful ways.

Digital communication creates the illusion of closeness, but often without the depth. A heart emoji isn't the same as a hug. A "like" isn't the same as listening. And while technology can be a bridge, it can also be a barrier, especially when it replaces face-to-face interaction or distracts us from the people right in front of us.

I'm not saying technology is bad. It can absolutely support connection when used intentionally. But it's no substitute for the kind of relationships that nourish us, those built on trust, vulnerability, and shared experience.

Why Connection Matters for Mental Health

Human beings are wired for connection. It's not a luxury, it's biological. From the moment we're born, we seek closeness, comfort, and belonging. Our nervous systems regulate through relationships. Our brains thrive on social interaction. And our hearts heal in the presence of others.

The Harvard Study of Adult Development, which has followed participants for over 80 years, found that the quality of our relationships is the strongest predictor of happiness and longevity. Not wealth. Not fame. Not achievement. Connection.

Loneliness, on the other hand, is devastating. Research shows that chronic isolation is as harmful to health as smoking 15 cigarettes a day. It increases stress, weakens the immune system, and raises the risk of depression and anxiety. And it's not just about how many people you know, it's about how deeply you feel known.

Connection reduces stress. It boosts mood. It helps us feel safe, seen, and supported. And it reminds us that we're not alone in our struggles.

The Purpose of This Book

Everything we've explored so far, mindfulness, nourishment, movement, sleep, boundaries, and habits, has been building toward this truth: you are not alone.

You were never meant to carry everything by yourself. But in order to connect meaningfully with others, you need capacity. You need energy, clarity, and emotional bandwidth. That's why we started with self-care, because you can't pour from an empty cup. You can't show up for others when you're depleted. And you can't heal in isolation.

This chapter is about connection; how to build it, nurture it, and lean on it when you need it most. It's about recognizing that asking for support isn't weakness, it's wisdom. It's about understanding the different types of relationships in your life, and how each one plays a role in your mental health.

We'll explore how to deepen existing relationships, how to create new ones, and how to know when it's time to seek professional support. Because sometimes, what you need isn't advice, it's presence. Someone to sit with you in the dark until the light returns.

Let's explore how to build and nurture the connections that sustain us, starting close and moving outward.

The Concentric Circles of Connection

Not all relationships are created equal. Some people know your soul. Others know your coffee order. Both matter but in very different ways. Understanding the layers of connection in your life helps you invest your energy wisely, set healthy boundaries, and build the kind of support system that truly sustains you.

The Framework: Circles of Connection

Imagine your relationships as concentric circles, radiating outward from you at the center. Each circle represents a different level of closeness, trust, and emotional investment. This framework isn't rigid, it's fluid. People can move between circles over time. But having clarity about where someone currently belongs helps you relate to them in a way that's appropriate and sustainable.

Circle 1: Intimate Partners / Closest Relationships

This is your innermost circle: your spouse, life partner, or maybe one or two people who know you completely. These are the people you can be vulnerable with, without fear of judgment. They've seen your flaws, your fears, your messy moments and they stay. These relationships require the most time, energy, and honesty. They're your emotional home base.

Circle 2: Family

This includes your immediate family and possibly close extended relatives. These relationships are often lifelong, shaped by shared history and deep emotional ties. Family can be a source of profound support or profound stress. Sometimes both. Navigating this circle requires grace, boundaries, and a clear understanding of what's healthy for you.

Circle 3: Close Friends

These are the people you call when something significant happens, good or bad. They know your story, your struggles, your dreams. You trust them with your fears and failures. These friendships are chosen, not inherited, and they often reflect your values and growth. Most people have between three and eight close friends. These relationships are gold.

Circle 4: Friends and Regular Connections

This wider circle includes people you genuinely enjoy but don't share everything with—colleagues you're close to, neighbors you trust, members of your book club or faith community. These relationships contribute to your sense of belonging. They may not be deeply intimate, but they're still meaningful.

Circle 5: Acquaintances

This broader circle includes people you know casually but positively—the barista who remembers your order, the person you chat with at the gym, the friendly coworker from another department. These "weak ties" matter more than we think. They create the social fabric of your life and can offer surprising moments of connection.

Circle 6: Strangers / Community

This outermost circle includes everyone else—people you pass on the street and the broader community you're part of. Even these fleeting interactions can be meaningful. A kind word, a shared smile, a moment of generosity; they remind us that we're part of something larger than ourselves.

Here's the key insight: you don't need deep connection with everyone. But you do need some deep connections, and a sense of broader community. Both are essential for mental and emotional health.

Understanding Your Circles

Not all circles are equal and that's okay. Your innermost circles require the most vulnerability and energy. Your outer circles provide variety, perspective, and a sense of place. Problems arise when we confuse the circles, expecting inner-circle intimacy from outer-circle people or keeping everyone at arm's length out of fear or exhaustion.

Some common mistakes we all make in truly understanding our circles include treating everyone like an inner-circle person. This leads to burnout and boundary violations. Not everyone is meant to hold your deepest truths. Keeping everyone in the outer circles. This creates isolation. You need people who know the real you. Expecting acquaintances to provide the support only close friends can. It's not fair to them or to you. And finally, oversharing with people who haven't earned that trust. Vulnerability is powerful, but it needs to be safe.

The goal is to know which circle each person occupies and relate to them accordingly. This doesn't mean being cold or calculating, it means being wise with your emotional energy.

One person I worked with realized she was treating coworkers like close friends or even family, sharing intimate struggles, venting about personal issues, and expecting deep emotional support. When those relationships didn't reciprocate, she felt hurt and rejected. She complained to me about it, saying, "But everyone thinks of each other as family here!" Not me and apparently not everyone else. Once she took a closer look at the relationships that actually existed, she found appropriate support elsewhere, and eventually the work relationships improved.

I'm always cautious when people say, 'My kid's school is like a family.' Or, 'My church is my family.' I hate to tell you this, but they are not. Organizations use "family" language to create loyalty and discourage boundaries, but that doesn't make it true. Yes, individuals can move in and out of the circles, but it is unwise to call someone your BFF before you've checked with them!

Assessing Your Circles

Take a moment to reflect. Ask yourself:

Who is in my innermost circle? If the answer is "no one," that's important information. Not a judgment, just a signal that something needs attention.

Do I have close friends I can be fully honest with?

Are my circles balanced, or am I isolated in one area?

Am I investing energy in relationships that truly matter?

Are there relationships that are draining me, and maybe belong in an outer circle or outside my circles entirely?

Here's a reality check: If you can't name 2–3 people you could call at 3 AM in a crisis, your inner circles need care. That doesn't mean you've failed, it means you're human. And it's fixable.

Building connection takes time, intention, and courage. But it starts with clarity. When you understand your circles, you can begin to nurture the relationships that sustain you and release the ones that don't.

Nurturing Your Inner Circles

The people closest to you are your anchors. They're the ones who hold your story, witness your growth, and walk with you through joy and pain. These relationships, your inner circles, don't just happen. They're built. They're maintained. And they require care, attention, and intention.

Let's explore how to strengthen and sustain these essential connections.

Circle 1: Intimate Partnerships

Intimate partnerships, whether with a spouse, life partner, or someone you share your deepest life with, are the most emotionally demanding and rewarding relationships we have. They sit at the center of your connection circles, and when they're strong, they can be a source of profound stability. When neglected, they can become a source of deep pain.

What makes these relationships work isn't perfection, it's presence and the ability to be honest without cruelty, vulnerable without fear, and consistent even when life gets messy. It's the willingness to repair when things go wrong, not just sweep them under the rug.

Common challenges creep in quietly. We start taking each other for granted. Conversations become transactional, "Did you pay the electric bill?" "Can you pick up the kids?" Emotional intimacy gets pushed aside because life is busy. We assume they "just know" what we need, instead of saying it out loud.

Here are a few practical ways to nurture this circle:

- Weekly check-ins. Set aside 20–30 minutes to talk beyond logistics. Ask each other, "How are you really doing?" "What's been hard this week?" "What's been good?" These conversations build emotional intimacy and keep you connected.

- Express appreciation regularly. Say thank you for the small things. "I noticed you handled dinner when I was overwhelmed. That meant a lot." Gratitude keeps resentment from building.
- Repair quickly. Conflict is inevitable. What matters is how you handle it. "I'm sorry I snapped at you. I was stressed, but that's not an excuse. How can I make this right?" Owning your part and making amends strengthens trust.
- Protect the relationship from stress. When life gets overwhelming, don't let your partner become the emotional dumping ground. Say, "I need to vent for five minutes. Can I do that, and then we talk about something lighter?" This creates space for both support and relief.

I've seen couples come back from the brink simply by recommitting to weekly date nights and honest conversations. One couple I worked with had drifted into roommate mode, coexisting but disconnected. When they started carving out intentional time together, their relationship transformed. Not overnight, but steadily.

Circle 2: Family Connections

Family is complicated. You don't choose your family, but you do choose how to relate to them. Some families are sources of deep support. Others are sources of stress. And sometimes, they're both.

When family relationships are healthy, they can be deeply grounding. But they still require intentional effort. Staying connected means more than showing up for holidays or sending birthday texts.

Try this:

Stay connected intentionally. Call regularly, not just out of obligation. Ask real questions: "What's been on your mind lately?" Share your own life, too. Let them see you.

Create new traditions. You don't have to repeat childhood patterns. Build rituals that reflect who you are now: Sunday dinners, annual trips, group texts with photos. These traditions create shared meaning.

But what if family relationships are difficult?

Set boundaries without guilt. As we discussed in Chapter 5, you're allowed to limit contact with family members who are toxic, critical, or draining. You can love someone from a distance. Boundaries protect your peace.

Grieve what isn't. Some families will never be what you wish they were. That grief is real. Naming it helps you move forward without pretending.

Build chosen family. Close friends can become family. The people who show up, who see you, who celebrate and support you, they count. They're just as real, just as valuable. Several of our adult sons and their friends enthusiastically celebrate a Friendsgiving. They are young professionals, and making time for their DNA family is sometimes difficult over a short holiday. These events bond them to each other in a way that is modern, reciprocal, and healthy.

I know someone who grew up in a chaotic household. As an adult, she set firm boundaries with her parents and siblings. It wasn't easy, but it was necessary. Over time, she built a chosen family, friends who became her emotional home. She created the kind of support system she never had growing up.

Circle 3: Close Friendships

Close friends are the people who choose you, and you choose them. They're not bound by blood or obligation. They're bound by trust, shared experience, and mutual care. These relationships are among the most powerful predictors of happiness and life satisfaction.

But adult friendships are hard. Life gets busy. People move. Schedules conflict. Energy is limited. Without intention, even the best friendships can drift.

Here's how to build and maintain close friendships:

Prioritize consistency over intensity. You don't need weekly hangouts. You need regular contact. A simple text, "Thinking of you. How's that work thing going?" can keep the connection alive. A monthly coffee or walk builds trust over time.

Be the friend you want to have. Show up when they're struggling. Celebrate their wins without jealousy. Listen without trying to fix. Forgive small slights. Friendship is a two-way street.

Be vulnerable first. Friendship deepens when someone takes the risk of honesty. Share something real: "I've been struggling with anxiety lately." Vulnerability invites vulnerability.

Make time, even when it's hard. Put it on the calendar. Treat friend time as non-negotiable, like a doctor's appointment. Even 30 minutes matters. It's not about the length of time, it's about the intention.

One of the more difficult, but very freeing things to do, is to let go of friendships that have run their course. Not all friendships last forever. Some are for a season; some are for a lifetime. You can love someone and still release the friendship. It's okay to move on.

Try a friendship audit, or "friendventory". Make a list of who energizes you, who drains you, who do you trust with hard things, and who shows up consistently. Ask yourself if you're investing in the friendships that matter.

One person I know realized their "best friend" from college had become more of an obligation than a connection. Every interaction felt forced. They let that friendship fade and invested more in a newer relationship that felt alive and reciprocal. It wasn't easy, but it was freeing, and ultimately, healing.

Your inner circles are sacred. They're where you're seen, supported, and strengthened. They don't require perfection, but they do require presence. When you nurture these relationships, you create a foundation of connection that can carry you through anything.

Beyond your closest circles, there are people who can guide you through specific challenges, mentors, coaches, and those who've walked the path before you.

The Power of Guides and Mentors

You don't have to figure it all out alone.

Whatever you're facing, whether it's a career crossroads, a parenting challenge, a creative block, or a season of emotional struggle, someone else has walked that path before you. They've stumbled, learned, grown, and come out the other side with wisdom to share. Their experience can save you years of trial and error. And sometimes, they can see things in you that you can't yet see in yourself.

Mentors and guides aren't just for professional development. They're for life. They help us grow, reflect, and stay grounded. They offer perspective when we're stuck, encouragement when we're unsure, and clarity when we're overwhelmed.

There are many types of guides:

Formal mentors: someone in your field or life stage who offers structured guidance. Think of a senior colleague, a seasoned parent, or a community leader.

Informal mentors: people you admire and learn from through observation and conversation. They may not even know they're mentoring you.

Coaches: professionals who help you achieve specific goals, whether in career, wellness, relationships, or personal growth.

Elders and wise voices: those further along in life who offer perspective, calm, and the long view.

These relationships don't have to be lifelong or intense. Sometimes, a single conversation with the right person can shift your entire trajectory.

Finding and Working with Mentors

So how do you find a mentor?

Start by looking for someone who's 5–10 years ahead of where you want to be. Not so far ahead that they've forgotten what it's like to be in your shoes, but far enough to offer meaningful perspective. Notice who you're drawn to, whose life, work, or character you admire. That's often a clue.

When you're ready to reach out, be clear and respectful. Perhaps say, "I really admire how you've navigated your career and kept your values intact. Would you be open to meeting for coffee once a month? I'd love to learn from your experience."

Make it easy for them. Come with specific questions. Respect their time. Follow through on their advice. And let them know how their guidance has helped you. Mentorship is a gift, showing appreciation keeps it alive.

Here are a few great questions to ask a mentor:

"What do you wish you'd known at my stage?"

"What mistakes did you make that I can avoid?"

"How did you handle [specific challenge]?"

"What books or resources shaped your thinking?"

I once worked with a young teacher who sought out a veteran educator as a mentor. They met monthly over coffee, talking about classroom management, work-life balance, and how to stay grounded in the chaos of school life. One conversation, in particular, changed her perspective: when she confessed she felt like a failure after a difficult parent meeting, her mentor shared that she'd had the same experience—and taught her how to set boundaries with parents while maintaining professionalism. That mentorship didn't just improve her teaching—it helped her feel less alone, more confident, and more connected to her purpose. Many schools have formal mentoring programs to assist new teachers.

Another person I know was in a career transition and felt completely lost. They hired a coach who helped them clarify their values, explore new paths, and take action. Within six months, they had a new job, a renewed sense of direction, and a toolkit for future decisions.

Being a Mentor

You don't have to be an expert to guide someone. If you're even one step ahead, you have something to offer. Sharing what you've learned helps solidify it and mentoring is often reciprocal. You learn as much as you teach.

Being a good mentor isn't about having all the answers. It's about listening, sharing your story, and creating space for someone else to grow.

Here's how to be a thoughtful mentor:

Listen more than you advise—sometimes people just need to be heard. Share your failures, not just your successes; that's where the real learning lives. Ask questions that help them think: 'What feels most important to you right now?' or 'What's one small step you could take?' Celebrate their wins and let them know you see their progress. Finally, give them permission to take a different path—your way isn't the only way.

I've mentored young educators, workshop participants, and colleagues navigating big life changes. One of the most meaningful experiences was walking alongside a coworker going through a divorce. I didn't have all the answers, but I listened, shared my own story, and reminded them they weren't alone. That connection helped both of us grow.

Mentors and guides are part of the human connection we all need. They remind us that growth is possible, that wisdom is shared, and that we're never truly alone on the journey.

Talking to Trusted People

One of the most powerful tools for mental health is simply this: talking to someone you trust.

It sounds simple, almost too simple. But speaking your struggles aloud can be transformative. When you name what's weighing on you, it often becomes less overwhelming. Saying it out loud shrinks the monster in your mind. You gain perspective, hearing yourself helps you see things more clearly. You feel less alone, someone is witnessing your pain, not trying to fix it, just being with you in it. And often, you discover solutions you couldn't see on your own.

But talking only helps if you talk to the right people. Not everyone is equipped to hold space for your vulnerability. Some will meet you with compassion. Others, unintentionally or not, will make you feel worse. Learning to identify safe people and how to ask for support is a skill worth cultivating.

Who to Talk To (and Who to Avoid)

Let's break it down into three categories: green light, yellow light, and red light people.

Green Light People are the ones you can trust with your heart. They listen without judgment. They keep your confidences. They don't try to "fix" you unless you ask. They validate your feelings, even if they don't fully understand. They offer perspective, not platitudes.

These are the people who make you feel lighter after talking. You leave the conversation feeling seen, heard, and supported.

Yellow Light People mean well, but they're not always safe for deep sharing. They tend to minimize: "It's not that bad." They make it about themselves: "When that happened to me..." They give unsolicited advice. They struggle with boundaries and might share your story.

You can still talk to yellow light people, but proceed with caution. Share selectively. Notice how you feel afterward. If you feel dismissed or drained, it's okay to pull back.

Red Light People are the ones to avoid when you're vulnerable. They gossip. They judge or shame. They weaponize your vulnerability later. They make you feel worse after talking.

It's painful to realize someone you care about isn't safe for emotional sharing. But protecting your mental health means being honest about who can hold space and who can't.

How to Identify Safe People

Start small. Share something mildly personal and watch how they respond. Do they listen? Do they respect your privacy? Do they follow up later with care? If so, you can share more. Trust is earned gradually, not given all at once.

How to Ask for Support

Sometimes we struggle not because we lack support—but because we don't know how to ask for it. Here's the difference between a vague ask and a clear one: Vague ask: "I'm really struggling." Why this doesn't work: This leaves the other person guessing. Do you want to talk? Do you need help? Are you okay?

169

Clear ask: "I'm overwhelmed with work and need to vent for 10 minutes. Can I do that, or is now not a good time?" "I'm going through something hard and I need advice. Do you have 30 minutes this week?" "I don't need solutions, I just need you to listen. Can we talk?"

When someone offers help, let them help. Don't default to "I'm fine." Be specific: "Could you pick up my kid from school Tuesday?" Then say thank you. And when they need support, reciprocate. That's how trust deepens.

What to Do When Someone Dismisses You

Not everyone will respond well. If someone minimizes your pain or shifts the focus to themselves, remember: their response is about them, not you.

You can say, "I don't think you understand what I'm saying. This is really important to me." If they still don't get it, try someone else. Not everyone can hold space for hard things and that's okay. Keep looking. The right people are out there.

I once knew someone who kept their struggle private for months. They felt ashamed, afraid of being a burden. Finally, they told a trusted friend. That conversation changed everything. The friend didn't fix it but they listened, they cared, and they reminded them they weren't alone. That moment became a turning point.

Reconnecting After Distance

Sometimes the people you need are people you've drifted from. Life gets busy. Time passes. But that doesn't mean the connection is lost.

It's okay to reach out after months or even years. You can say, "Hey, I know it's been a while. I've been thinking about you and would love to catch up. Can we grab coffee?" You don't need to apologize for the gap. A simple, "Life got busy, and I let too much time pass. I'm sorry for that. I've missed you," is enough.

Sometimes the reconnection is easy. True friends can pick up where they left off, no resentment, just joy. Sometimes it's not. People change. The friendship might not fit anymore. That's okay. You can honor what was without forcing what isn't.

A former manager of mine reconnected with a college friend after ten years. They met for lunch, expecting it to be awkward. Instead, it felt like coming home. That friendship became a lifeline during a hard season. On the flip side, I've seen people reach out only to realize the connection had faded. They let it go with grace, grateful for what it once was.

Talking to trusted people is one of the most healing things you can do. It doesn't require a solution. It doesn't require a plan. It just requires presence, yours and theirs. When you speak your truth and someone holds it with care, something shifts. You feel less alone. You feel more whole. And that's where healing begins.

Support Groups – You're Not Alone

Sometimes the most powerful connection comes from people who truly understand what you're going through.

When you're facing something specific—grief, addiction, chronic illness, parenting challenges, divorce—it can feel isolating. Friends may care, but they might not fully get it. You can feel like you're speaking a language no one else understands. That's where support groups come in.

There's something profoundly healing about sitting in a room (or logging into a space) with people who've lived what you're living. You don't have to explain every detail. You don't have to justify your feelings. You're met with nods of recognition, not confusion. You realize you're not broken, not weak, and definitely not alone.

The right support groups offer a great deal, including:

- Shared experience: You're among people who've walked a similar path
- No explanation needed: They understand without a lengthy backstory
- Normalized struggle: You see that what you're feeling is human
- Practical wisdom: You hear what helped others—and what didn't
- Accountability and hope: Seeing others further along gives you perspective and encouragement"

Types of Support Groups

There are support groups for nearly every life challenge. Some are peer-led, some are professionally facilitated.

12-Step Programs

These include Alcoholics Anonymous (AA), Narcotics Anonymous (NA), Al-Anon (for families of addicts), and many others. They're widely available, peer-led, and built around a structured framework of recovery. While they include a spiritual component, many groups are flexible and inclusive of different beliefs.

Grief and Loss Groups

Hospices often offer free grief support groups. Programs like GriefShare (faith-based) and The Dinner Party (for young adults who've lost someone) create safe spaces to process loss and find connection.

Mental Health Support Groups

Organizations like NAMI (National Alliance on Mental Illness) and DBSA (Depression and Bipolar Support Alliance) offer groups for people living with mental health conditions. There are also groups focused on anxiety, OCD, and trauma recovery.

Parenting and Family Groups

Groups like MOPS (Mothers of Preschoolers) offer support for new parents. There are also groups for parents of children with ADHD, autism, or other special needs, as well as support for adoptive and foster families.

Chronic Illness and Disability Groups

Whether you're living with cancer, diabetes, lupus, or chronic pain, there are disease-specific groups that offer education and emotional support. Caregiver support groups are also available for those caring for loved ones with long-term conditions.

Life Transition Groups

Major life changes—divorce, job loss, retirement, becoming an empty nester—can be disorienting. Support groups help you work through these transitions with others who understand the emotional terrain.

Online Communities

When in-person groups aren't accessible, online communities can be a lifeline. Facebook groups, Reddit forums, and Discord servers offer 24/7 support. While they may lack the intimacy of face-to-face interaction, they still provide connection, advice, and a sense of belonging.

How to Find and Join a Group

You don't have to search alone. Here are some places to start:

Psychology Today has a searchable support group directory.

Hospitals and community centers often host groups.

Religious organizations (churches, synagogues, mosques) may offer or know of groups.

Try searching online: "[your issue] support group near me."

What to Expect

Most groups are free or low-cost. They typically meet weekly or biweekly for 1–2 hours. Confidentiality is key; what's said in the group stays in the group. And you don't have to share right away. Listening is okay. Many people attend their first few meetings just to observe and get comfortable.

Not every group will feel right. That's normal. The fit matters. If one doesn't work, try another. The right group can feel like a lifeline.

I once knew someone who joined a grief group after losing a parent. They were hesitant at first, unsure if it would help. But sitting with others who understood, who had cried the same tears, asked the same questions, felt the same ache, made them feel less alone. That group became a place of healing, not just for grief, but for connection.

A close family member in recovery credits their 12-step group with saving their life. It wasn't just the structure, it was the people. The shared stories. The honesty. The hope.

And in my own work with workshop groups, I've seen how strangers can become allies. When people gather with intention and openness, something sacred happens. Walls come down. Support rises up.

Support groups remind us of a simple truth: you are not alone. Whatever you're facing, someone else has faced it too. And together, healing becomes possible.

Professional Help – Therapy, Counseling, and Beyond

Sometimes the support we need is professional. And that's not just okay, it's wise.

We live in a culture that often celebrates independence and self-reliance. But mental health isn't something you "power through." You don't have to wait until you're in crisis to seek help. Therapy isn't just for "serious" problems, it's for anyone who wants to understand themselves better, process emotions, or build healthier habits and relationships.

Professional help offers something unique: trained guidance. Therapists, counselors, coaches, and other professionals are equipped to help you stand up to life's challenges with tools, insight, and compassion. They're not there to judge or fix you; they're there to walk with you, ask the right questions, and help you find your way forward.

We're gradually becoming more accepting of therapy and mental health care. It's no longer taboo. In fact, I know quite a few people who proudly share how therapy is transforming their lives.

This cultural shift matters. The more we normalize seeking help, the more lives we save.

When to Seek Professional Help

You don't need a diagnosis to benefit from therapy. You don't need to hit rock bottom. You just need to recognize that something isn't working and that you're ready for support.

Consider professional help if your struggles are persistent, lasting weeks or months or if they're interfering with daily life: work, relationships, self-care. You might also consider therapy if you've tried other strategies and still feel stuck or if you want guidance from someone trained to help.

If you're having thoughts of self-harm or suicide, please seek professional help immediately.

There are many common reasons people seek therapy, including, anxiety, depression, trauma; grief and loss; relationship issues; life transitions (career change, divorce, becoming a parent); stress management; building self-esteem; and processing childhood experiences.

Therapy is not a sign of weakness, it's a sign of courage. It's saying, "I care enough about myself to get help."

Types of Professional Help

There's no one-size-fits-all approach. Different professionals offer different kinds of support, depending on your needs.

Therapists and Counselors

These are licensed professionals such as LCSWs (Licensed Clinical Social Workers), LPCs (Licensed Professional Counselors), LMFTs (Licensed Marriage and Family Therapists), and psychologists who provide talk therapy. They use various approaches like CBT (Cognitive Behavioral Therapy), EMDR (Eye Movement Desensitization and Reprocessing), psychodynamic therapy, and more. You can work with them individually, as a couple, or as a family.

Psychiatrists

Psychiatrists are medical doctors who specialize in mental health. They can diagnose conditions and prescribe medication. Often, they work alongside therapists to provide comprehensive care.

Life Coaches

Coaches focus on goals, motivation, and forward movement. They're great for career transitions, productivity, and personal development. However, they're not licensed to treat mental health conditions and shouldn't be used as a substitute for therapy when deeper emotional work is needed.

Pastoral Counselors

For those who want to integrate faith and therapy, pastoral counselors offer spiritual perspective alongside psychological support. They're often trained in both theology and counseling.

Group Therapy

Led by a licensed therapist, group therapy is more structured than support groups. It combines professional guidance with peer support and can be incredibly powerful for issues like addiction, trauma, or social anxiety.

How to Find a Therapist

Finding the right therapist can feel daunting, but there are many resources to help you get started.

Where to Look:

Insurance directory: Check who's in-network.

Psychology Today: Search by location, issue, and specialty.

Open Path Collective: Offers affordable therapy ($30–$80/session).

BetterHelp, Talkspace: Online therapy platforms.

EAP (Employee Assistance Program): Many workplaces offer 3–6 free sessions.

Community mental health centers: Often offer sliding scale fees.

What to Look For:

Licensed and credentialed

Specializes in your issue (e.g., trauma, anxiety, relationships)

Therapy approach that resonates with you

Someone you feel comfortable with—trust your gut

The First Session:

Think of it as an interview. Ask:

"What's your approach to therapy?"

"Have you worked with [specific issue]?"

"What can I expect from sessions?"

"How do you measure progress?"

If it doesn't feel right, try someone else. Fit matters. You don't have to stay with the first therapist you try.

What Therapy Can (and Can't) Do

Therapy can:

> Help you understand patterns in your thinking and behavior

> Teach you coping skills and strategies

> Provide a safe space to process emotions

> Offer perspective and insight

> Hold you accountable to your goals

> Help you heal from past wounds

Therapy can't:

> Fix your problems for you—you do the work

> Make other people change

> Guarantee you'll never struggle again

> Replace medication when it's needed (though it can complement it)

The real work happens between sessions. Therapy gives you tools; you use them in daily life. Change takes time, practice, and patience. Be gentle with yourself.

Addressing Common Barriers

"I can't afford it."

Many therapists offer sliding scale fees.

EAPs, community centers, and Open Path Collective make therapy more accessible.

Some churches offer free counseling.

Online therapy is often more affordable.

Your mental health is worth the investment.

"I don't have time."

Many therapists offer evening or weekend appointments.

Online therapy eliminates commute time.

One hour a week is an investment in your well-being.

Ask yourself: What are you spending time on that matters less?

"What will people think?"

You don't owe anyone an explanation.

Seeing a therapist is as normal as seeing a doctor.

People who judge therapy often need it most.

"I should be able to handle this myself."

You see a doctor for physical health. A therapist is for mental health.

Asking for help is strength, not weakness.

Everyone needs support sometimes.

I've known people who resisted therapy for years. They thought they should be able to "figure it out." When they finally went, they said the same thing: "I wish I'd started sooner." Therapy didn't fix everything overnight, but it gave them clarity, tools, and a safe space to heal.

Professional help is not a last resort, it's a powerful resource. Whether you're navigating a crisis or simply want to grow, therapy can be a life-changing step toward clarity, resilience, and peace.

Closing: You Are Not Alone

This book has been about managing stress, caring for yourself, and building healthy habits. But all of that exists within the context of relationship. Because no matter how strong, independent, or capable you are, you are not meant to do life alone.

Connection is not optional. It's essential to your mental health, to your resilience, to your sense of purpose and meaning, and to your ability to weather hard seasons.

You don't need a huge social circle. You don't need to be the life of the party or have dozens of close friends. You just need a few people who really see you. You need to feel part of something larger than yourself. You need to know that someone has your back especially when life gets hard.

This chapter has given you a map:

- Know your circles and invest accordingly
- Nurture your closest relationships
- Find mentors and be a mentor
- Talk to trusted people
- Join support groups when you need shared experience
- Seek professional help without shame

And along the way, you've been given permission:

You are allowed to need people

You are allowed to ask for help

You are allowed to let go of relationships that hurt you

You are allowed to build the community you need

Connection is reciprocal. When you allow yourself to be supported, you give others the gift of being needed. When you offer support, you strengthen your own resilience. Connection is a two-way street—both giving and receiving matter.

So as you move forward, remember this:

You are not a burden. You are not too much. You are not alone. And the people who love you want to walk with you— through the hard and the beautiful, the grief and the joy. Let them.

You've done the work to care for yourself. Now, let that care extend outward. Build the connections that sustain you. And know, deep in your bones, that you are worthy of love, support, and belonging.

Connection sustains us. But how we think about our challenges, the stories we tell ourselves, also shapes our resilience. Let's explore the power of perspective and positivity.

Reflection Questions:

- Who is in my innermost circle? If I can't name 2-3 people, what does that tell me?
- Which relationships give me energy? Which drain me?
- Am I investing in the connections that matter most to me?
- Is there someone I've drifted from that I want to reconnect with?
- What stops me from asking for help when I need it?
- Have I considered joining a support group or seeing a therapist? If not, why?
- Who in my life needs my support right now?
- What would change if I let people see me, really see me?

Instruction: Choose one or two questions. Write honestly. If the answers reveal a need for change, that's not failure, it's clarity. And clarity is the first step toward connection.

Map Your Circles:

Draw concentric circles on a piece of paper. Place yourself in the center. Then write names in each circle:

Circle 1 (Intimate): Who can you be completely yourself with?

Circle 2 (Family): Who is family, by blood or choice?

Circle 3 (Close Friends): Who knows your story and shows up consistently?

Circle 4 (Friends/Regular Connections): Who do you enjoy and trust?

Circle 5 (Acquaintances): Who adds positive energy to your life?

After mapping, reflect:

- ❑ Are my circles balanced or heavily weighted in one area?
- ❑ Are there people in outer circles I wish were closer?
- ❑ Are there people in inner circles who shouldn't be?
- ❑ Do I have enough depth in my inner circles?
- ❑ What's one action I can take this week to strengthen a connection that matters?

Sometimes we just need someone to simply be there—not to fix anything, but to let us feel we're supported and not alone.

The Power of Positivity

Optimism is the faith that leads to achievement. Nothing can be done without hope and confidence. (Keller)

We live in a world that constantly tells us to "look on the bright side." Social media feeds overflow with inspirational quotes, cheerful affirmations, and the ever-present mantra: "Good vibes only." But beneath the surface of this positivity culture, many people are quietly struggling—feeling unseen, unheard, and invalidated.

There's a pressure to be positive that can feel suffocating. Imagine someone going through a painful divorce, barely holding it together, and being told, "Everything happens for a reason!" Instead of comfort, they feel dismissed. Instead of hope, they feel shame for not being able to smile through the pain. This is the shadow side of positivity, what we now call toxic positivity.

But positivity itself isn't the problem. It's how we use it.

There are two sides to positivity. Real positivity acknowledges hardship while maintaining hope. It says, "This is hard, and I believe I can get through it." It empowers. Toxic positivity, on the other hand, denies reality and invalidates emotions. It says, "Don't feel that. Just be happy." It gaslights. The goal isn't to be positive all the time, it's to choose your perspective when possible, in a way that honors both truth and hope.

This chapter isn't about forced cheerfulness or pretending everything is fine. It's about cultivating realistic optimism; the kind that sees possibilities without denying difficulties. It's about practicing gratitude as a grounding habit, not a performance. It's about celebrating progress, not just perfection. And it's about learning to choose your battles wisely, knowing when to lean into hope and when to simply sit with what is.

The balance we're seeking is gentle and honest:

Acknowledge the hard without drowning in it

Find meaning without forcing a silver lining

Practice gratitude without bypassing grief

Maintain hope without denying reality

Positivity, when rooted in truth, can be a powerful force for resilience. It doesn't erase pain, it helps us carry it with grace.

Let's explore how to cultivate genuine positivity, the kind that sustains you through hard seasons without asking you to pretend they're easy.

Positivity vs. Toxic Positivity

Before we talk about cultivating positivity, we need to talk about what it's not.

We've all heard the phrases: "Just stay positive!" "Everything happens for a reason." "Good vibes only." These messages are everywhere: from social media captions to well-meaning friends trying to help. But sometimes, instead of lifting us up, they leave us feeling worse. Why? Because they don't make space for what's real.

What Is Toxic Positivity?

Toxic positivity is the excessive and ineffective overgeneralization of a happy, optimistic state. It's the kind of positivity that denies, minimizes, or invalidates authentic human emotions in favor of a cheerful façade. It's not about hope, it's about avoidance.

What does toxic positivity sound like? It's the phrases we've all heard: 'Just stay positive!' 'Everything happens for a reason.' 'Good vibes only.' 'At least it's not worse.' 'Look on the bright side.' 'Don't be so negative.' 'Just choose to be happy.' These messages might be well-intentioned, but they can be deeply harmful especially when someone is in pain.

In my personal experience as an educator, I tried to refrain from building false hope in my students. The wishful adage that, "You can be anything you want to be!", falls short as a promise when someone with diabetes dreams of one day being a pilot. We've all heard that where there is no vision, people perish. That might be true; however, somehow, that vision must be grounded in rational thinking.

Why It's Harmful

Why is toxic positivity so harmful? First, it invalidates real emotions, your pain is real, and pretending it's not doesn't make it go away. It creates shame, making you feel like you're failing for not being happy enough. It prevents processing because you can't heal what you won't acknowledge. It damages relationships because people stop sharing honestly when they're met with dismissive positivity. And it increases isolation; you feel like you have to hide your struggles to be accepted.

Imagine someone who just lost their job. They're scared, uncertain, and grieving the loss of stability. A friend says, "Everything happens for a reason! This is just the universe redirecting you!" Instead of comfort, they feel dismissed. What they needed was, "This sucks. I'm sorry. How can I help?"

Or someone grieving a miscarriage being told, "At least you can try again!" That may be true, but the loss they're feeling right now is real and deserves to be honored. Toxic positivity skips over the pain and rushes to the silver lining often leaving the person feeling unseen.

What Is Genuine Positivity?

Genuine positivity acknowledges reality—including pain, loss, and difficulty—while still maintaining hope, looking for growth, and choosing constructive responses when possible. It doesn't deny the hard stuff. It walks with it.

What does genuine positivity sound like? It says things like, 'This is really hard. And you're handling it.' Or, 'I don't know why this happened, but I'm here with you.' It makes space with phrases like, 'It's okay to not be okay right now' and 'What do you need? I'm listening.' It holds complexity: 'You can feel sad and still have hope.' And it honors reality: 'Some days are just survival days, and that's enough.

Genuine positivity validates your emotions, they're real and appropriate. It creates space for healing because you process rather than suppress. It builds resilience because facing reality strengthens you more than denying it. It deepens relationships through honesty and real connection. And it allows for growth because you can't grow from something you won't acknowledge.

The key difference?

Toxic positivity says: "Don't feel bad."

Genuine positivity says: "It's okay to feel bad. And you'll get through this." Genuine positivity is grounded. It doesn't rush you. It doesn't shame you. It simply says, "I see you. I believe in you. And I'm here."

The Spectrum of Response

Not every situation requires positivity. Sometimes the most appropriate response is grief, anger, or sadness. The goal isn't to be cheerful, it's to be real.

Think of responses as a spectrum:

Denial / Toxic Positivity ←→ Realistic Acknowledgment ←→ Despair / Hopelessness

The healthiest place to land is in the middle: realistic acknowledgment. You see things as they are, feel what you feel, and still believe you can handle it or get help to handle it.

Here's what this looks like in real situations:

Lost a job:

Toxic positivity: "This is great! Now you can pursue your passion!"

Realistic: "This is scary and uncertain. I'm going to feel my feelings and then make a plan."

Despair: "My life is over. I'll never recover from this."

Relationship ended:

Toxic positivity: "You dodged a bullet! You're better off!"

Realistic: "This hurts. I loved them. And eventually, I'll heal."

Despair: "I'll never find love again. I'm unlovable."

Chronic illness diagnosis:

Toxic positivity: "Your body is teaching you something! Be grateful!"

Realistic: "This changes things. I'm scared and sad. I'll figure out how to adapt."

Despair: "My life is ruined. There's no point in trying."

The middle path honors both pain and possibility. It doesn't rush you to feel better. It doesn't leave you stuck in hopelessness. It simply says, "This is hard. And you're not alone."

Gratitude as a Grounding Practice

One of the most powerful ways to cultivate genuine positivity is through gratitude. Not as a performance, but as a practice.

Gratitude isn't about pretending everything is fine. It's about learning to notice what's good even when life is hard. It's about anchoring yourself in small moments of beauty, kindness, and grace, especially when the big picture feels overwhelming. Gratitude doesn't erase pain, but it helps you carry it with more steadiness.

Why Gratitude Matters

The science is clear: gratitude rewires your brain. When practiced regularly, it helps you notice the good alongside the hard. It doesn't make problems disappear, but it shifts your perspective.

It reminds you that even in difficulty, there are still things worth holding onto.

Research shows that gratitude improves mood, sleep quality, relationships, and physical health. It's one of the most studied and effective interventions in positive psychology. And it's accessible to everyone, no special tools required.

But let's be clear about what gratitude is not. Gratitude is not: a denial of difficulty. ("I should just be grateful."), it is not a replacement for addressing real problems, it's not something you only feel when life is going well, nor is it a way to shame yourself for struggling.

Simply put, gratitude is a choice to notice what's working alongside what's not. It is a practice of paying attention to small goods and a way to train your brain to see possibilities. Finally, it is a grounding force when everything feels chaotic.

Gratitude is a both/and practice. You can be grateful for your home and stressed about the mortgage. You can be grateful for your health and struggling with chronic pain. You can be grateful for your partner and frustrated with them today. Gratitude doesn't erase complexity, it holds space for it.

How to Practice Gratitude

Daily Gratitude Journaling

One of the simplest and most effective ways to practice gratitude is through journaling. The practice is straightforward: write down 3–5 things you're grateful for each day.

Why does gratitude journaling work? It works because it trains your brain to notice positive details and creates a record you can revisit on hard days. It works because it takes less than five minutes and compounds over time—small shifts become big changes.

How can you do it well?

Be specific, not generic:

> Generic: 'I'm grateful for my family.'

> Specific: 'I'm grateful my son made me laugh this morning when he told me about his dream.'

Include the small stuff:

> Hot coffee. A text from a friend. The sun through the window. Clean sheets. A good parking spot. These matter. They add up.

Notice what's working, not just what's easy:

> 'I'm grateful my body got me through a hard workout today.'

> 'I'm grateful I had the courage to set a boundary.'

Don't force it on terrible days:

> Some days, 'I'm grateful I survived today' is enough. Some days, you skip it. That's okay."

I think often of my mother's gratitude journals. She started them during one of the hardest seasons of her life. Money was tight. Health was uncertain. But every night, she wrote down three things she was grateful for. Sometimes it was just "a warm blanket," "a kind nurse," or "a quiet moment." She used to say, "Gratitude can be everything when you have nothing." Her journals were proof that this practice transforms lives—especially in hard seasons.

Gratitude Letters

Another powerful practice is writing a letter of gratitude to someone who impacted your life. You don't have to send it (though you can). The act of writing is healing in itself.

How to do it:

Choose someone who helped, taught, or supported you. Write specifically about what they did and how it affected you. If you send it, you give them a gift. If you don't, you still benefit from reflecting on their impact.

Someone I know wrote a letter to a teacher from 20 years ago, thanking them for believing in them when no one else did. They sent it. The teacher cried and said it was the best thing that had happened to them that year. Both were changed by it.

Gratitude in Conversation

Gratitude doesn't have to be a solo practice. It can be woven into your relationships and daily routines. Try this at dinner: Everyone shares one good thing from their day. Or, before bed ask, "What was your favorite moment today?" With your partner, show weekly appreciation; tell each other one thing you're grateful for about them.

This practice strengthens relationships and shifts household culture toward noticing good. It creates a rhythm of reflection and connection.

Gratitude for Hard Things (With Caution)

This part is delicate. Gratitude for hard things is not about being grateful for the pain itself. It's about recognizing what the experience revealed or taught—when you're ready.

Not: "I'm grateful for my trauma." Trauma is not a gift. But: "I'm grateful I learned I'm stronger than I thought."

Not: "I'm grateful for my illness." Illness sucks. But: "I'm grateful for the people who showed up when I was sick."

This kind of gratitude should never be forced. It's not a shortcut to healing. It's a reflection that may come after the storm, not during it. And it's yours to name. No one else gets to decide when or how you find meaning.

Gratitude is not a magic fix. It's a daily anchor. A way to stay grounded in what's good, even when life is hard. It's not about pretending. It's about noticing. And over time, it can shift your perspective, soften your heart, and strengthen your resilience.

Celebrating Small Wins

Gratitude helps you notice what's good. But you also need to celebrate what you've accomplished even when it's small.

We're trained to celebrate only the big milestones: promotions, graduations, weddings, major achievements. These are the moments that get the applause, the social media posts, the champagne toasts. But life isn't made up of constant milestones. It's made up of small, unremarkable days—the kind where you quietly show up, do your best, and keep going.

If you only celebrate the big, you miss 99% of your life.

Why Small Wins Matter

Small wins are powerful. They build momentum. They remind you that you're capable. They create positive reinforcement; your brain starts to associate effort with reward. And they help you see progress, even when it feels invisible.

What counts as a small win? You got out of bed on a hard day. You went for a 10-minute walk. You ate a vegetable. You asked for help. You set a boundary. You didn't snap at your kid, even though you wanted to. You cried and then kept going. You showed up. These are not small. These are survival. These are strength. And they deserve to be acknowledged.

How to Celebrate Small Wins

Celebrating small wins doesn't require a party. It just requires attention. Here are a few ways to make it a habit:

Acknowledge Them Out Loud.

Say it: "I did it. I'm proud of myself." Tell someone: "I managed to [thing] today, and I'm really proud." Naming your wins gives them weight. It helps you internalize your progress.

Write Them Down

Keep a "wins journal" or add them to your gratitude practice. On hard days, read back through past wins. It's a reminder that you've done hard things before and you can do them again.

Create a Visual Tracker

Use checkboxes, stickers, or marks on a calendar. Seeing progress is motivating. It turns effort into something tangible.

Share Them

Text a friend: "Small win today: I actually cooked dinner instead of ordering out." Post in a supportive group, not for validation, but for celebration. Let others cheer you on. Let connection amplify your progress.

Give Yourself a Reward

Not "I earned this because I was good." But, "I'm celebrating myself because I showed up." Some examples may include: 20 minutes of guilt-free reading, taking an extra-long shower, or watching an episode of your favorite show.

The key: Don't wait for someone else to notice or celebrate you. You do it.

Reframing "Failure" as Data

Celebrating small wins also means learning to reframe failure. Because not everything goes as planned. And that's okay. Instead of: "I failed. I'm terrible at this." Try: "That didn't work. What can I learn?" Failure is feedback, not identity.

Examples

You skipped your workout for a week:

Toxic positivity: "It's fine! Just start fresh Monday!"

Beating yourself up: "I have no willpower. I'm lazy."

Realistic positivity: "I've been exhausted. My body needed rest. I can start again tomorrow."

You snapped at your kid:

> Toxic positivity: "Kids are resilient! They'll forget it!"

> Beating yourself up: "I'm a terrible parent."

> Realistic positivity: "I was overwhelmed and reacted poorly. I'll apologize and try again."

You didn't get the promotion:

> Toxic positivity: "The universe has something better planned!"

> Beating yourself up: "I'm not good enough."

> Realistic positivity: "That hurts. I worked hard. I'll ask for feedback and decide what's next."

One person I know trained for months to run a marathon. They were disciplined, focused, and excited. But two weeks before the race, they got injured. They couldn't finish. At first, they felt like a failure. But then they reframed it: they had trained for months, improved their fitness, built discipline, and learned about their body. The goal shifted but the wins were real. Six months later, they ran a different race, stronger and wiser for the experience.

Celebrating small wins is about honoring your effort, not just your outcomes. It's about recognizing that progress isn't always visible, and success isn't always loud. It's about choosing to see yourself as someone who is trying and that alone is worth celebrating.

Picking Your Battles

Positivity isn't about being happy all the time. It's about choosing where to invest your emotional energy.

You only have so much bandwidth. Your time, attention, and emotional reserves are finite. You can't care deeply about everything. You can't fix every problem. You can't win every argument. And when you try, you burn out.

The Cost of Fighting Every Fight

When you engage in every conflict, every annoyance, every injustice (big or small), the result is predictable:

Chronic stress and resentment

Weakened relationships

Loss of clarity about what actually matters

You end up exhausted, bitter, and disconnected from your values. The solution isn't apathy, it's discernment. It's learning to pick your battles.

How to Decide What's Worth Your Energy

Here are five questions to help you decide whether a situation deserves your emotional investment:

1. Does this align with my Main Thing?

(Callback to Chapter 4.)

If it doesn't serve your core values or priorities, let it go. Not everything is your mission.

2. Will this matter in a week? A month? A year?

> If not, it's probably not worth the fight. Time offers perspective. Don't sacrifice your peace for something fleeting.

3. Can I influence the outcome?

> If you have no control, engaging only drains you. (Remember the Quadrants from Chapter 4.) Focus on what you can change.

4. Is this about principles or pride?

> Sometimes we dig in because our ego is bruised, not because the issue truly matters. Be honest with yourself.

5. What's the cost of engaging vs. the cost of letting go?

> Which preserves your peace? Which honors your values? Choose accordingly.

Examples of Picking (and Not Picking) Battles

Let's look at some everyday situations and how to apply this framework.

At Work

> Let go: Your coworker's annoying habits: chewing loudly, messy desk.

> Engage: Your coworker taking credit for your work. That affects your integrity and reputation.

In Relationships

> Let go: How your partner loads the dishwasher.

Engage: Patterns of disrespect or broken trust. These impact emotional safety.

With Family

Let go: Your mom's opinions about your parenting, unless they're harmful.

Engage: Protecting your kids from toxic behavior or unsafe dynamics.

In Parenting

Let go: Your kid wearing mismatched clothes. (Remember the story from Chapter 4!)

Engage: Your kid being unkind to others. That's a values issue.

Online

Let go: Arguments with strangers on the internet. Almost always.

Engage: Advocating for causes that align with your values when you have capacity.

The principle is simple: Save your energy for what truly matters. Everything else is noise.

The Art of Letting Go

Some battles aren't yours to fight. And that's not weakness, it's wisdom.

You don't have to:

Correct every wrong opinion

Respond to every criticism

Fix every problem

Have the last word

Sometimes the strongest response is silence. Sometimes it's walking away. Sometimes it's saying, "I'm not engaging with this."

Letting go doesn't mean you don't care. It means you care enough about your peace, your purpose, and your relationships to choose wisely.

I once knew someone who argued with their father-in-law about politics at every family gathering. It never changed anyone's mind, it just ruined holidays. Eventually, they decided to stop engaging. Now they smile, change the subject, and preserve their peace. The relationship improved. The stress disappeared. And they realized: not every hill is worth dying on.

Picking your battles is an act of self-respect. It's how you protect your energy, your relationships, and your mental health. It's how you stay aligned with your values. And it's how you make space for the kind of positivity that's rooted in clarity not chaos.

Reframing Your Inner Narrative

The stories you tell yourself shape your reality. Let's explore how to reframe them.

We all have a running narrative in our minds about who we are, what we're capable of, and what our future holds. These stories aren't just background noise. They influence how we feel, how we act, and how we respond to challenges. Sometimes, those stories are empowering. But often, they're not.

Common negative narratives sound like this: 'I always fail.' 'Nothing ever works out for me.' 'I'm not good enough.' 'Everyone else has it figured out.' 'Things will never get better.' These stories feel true. But they're not facts, they're interpretations. And interpretations can be challenged, reshaped, and rewritten.

How to Challenge and Reframe Your Stories

Reframing your inner narrative isn't about lying to yourself or pretending everything is fine. It's about finding a more accurate, compassionate, and constructive way to talk to yourself.

Step 1: Notice the Story

Catch yourself in a negative narrative. Write it down. Naming it gives you power over it.

Step 2: Question It

Ask:

Is this absolutely true?

What's the evidence for and against it?

Am I catastrophizing or generalizing?

Most negative self-talk falls apart under scrutiny. It's often based on emotion, not fact.

Step 3: Reframe It

Find a more accurate, empowering story.

Example 1

Negative narrative: "I always fail at everything."

Challenge: Is that true? Have you never succeeded at anything?

Reframe: "Some things haven't worked out. I've also succeeded at [specific examples]. I'm learning."

Example 2

Negative narrative: "No one cares about me."

Challenge: Is that true? Can you name even one person who's shown they care?

Reframe: "I feel lonely right now. That doesn't mean I'm unloved. Sarah checked in on me last week. I'm not as alone as I feel."

Example 3

Negative narrative: "I'll never get through this."

Challenge: Have you survived hard things before?

Reframe: "This is really hard. And I've survived hard things before. I'll get through this too, one day at a time."

REBT Connection (Callback to Chapter 4)

This process is exactly what Rational Emotive Behavior Therapy (REBT) teaches: challenge irrational beliefs and replace them with rational ones.

Let's break it down:

Activating event: Didn't get the job

Belief: "I'm a failure. I'll never succeed."

Consequence: Depression, giving up

Now challenge the belief:

> "One rejection doesn't define me. Many successful people faced rejection."

> New belief: "This didn't work out. I'll keep trying."

> New consequence: Disappointment, but continued effort

This shift doesn't erase the pain but it redirects the story. It gives you a path forward.

The Power of "Yet"

One word can shift everything: yet.

> "I don't know how to do this" → "I don't know how to do this yet."

> "I'm not good at this" → "I'm not good at this yet."

> "This isn't working" → "This isn't working yet."

"Yet" implies:

> You're in process

> Growth is possible

> You haven't given up

This is the essence of a growth mindset, a concept developed by psychologist Carol Dweck. In a fixed mindset, you believe your abilities are static: "I can't." In a growth mindset, you believe they can develop: "I can't yet." That one word opens the door to possibility. It reminds you that you're not stuck, you're evolving.

Reframing your inner narrative is one of the most powerful tools for cultivating genuine positivity. It doesn't mean ignoring pain. It means telling the truth with hope. It means choosing stories that honor your struggle and your strength.

Realistic Hope

Positivity without hope is just pretending. Let's talk about cultivating realistic hope.

Hope is often misunderstood. It's not blind optimism. It's not pretending everything is fine. It's not wishful thinking with no action behind it. Real hope doesn't ignore pain, it walks alongside it.

What Is Realistic Hope?

Realistic hope is the belief that, even in the face of difficulty, something good is still possible. It's not a guarantee that everything will work out exactly how you want. It's the quiet conviction that you can influence outcomes, even if you can't control them. It's trusting that growth is possible, even in pain. It's choosing to keep moving forward, one step at a time.

Psychiatrist and Holocaust survivor Viktor Frankl wrote about this kind of hope in *Man's Search for Meaning*. He survived the unimaginable not by believing his suffering would magically end, but by finding meaning in it and choosing his response.

> "Everything can be taken from a man but one thing: the last of the human freedoms, to choose one's attitude in any given set of circumstances."

That's realistic hope. It's not about denying the darkness. It's about lighting a candle anyway.

How to Cultivate Realistic Hope

1. Focus on What You Can Control

(Callback to the Quadrants from Chapter 4.)

You can't control the economy, but you can update your resume. You can't control your diagnosis, but you can follow treatment and care for yourself. You can't control other people, but you can set boundaries.

Hope grows when you shift your energy toward what's within your reach.

2. Take One Small Action

Hope isn't just a feeling, it's a behavior. It grows through agency. Do something, even if it's tiny. Make the phone call. Take the walk. Ask for help. Show up.

Each small step is a vote for your future.

3. Connect with Others

(Tie back to Chapter 8.)

Hope is sustained in community. You don't have to do this alone. Talk to someone. Join a group. Let others remind you of your strength when you forget.

4. Look for Evidence of Past Resilience

You've survived every hard thing so far. That's not just a motivational quote—it's data. You're stronger than you think. Reflect on what you've overcome. Let it remind you that you can do hard things.

5. Allow Yourself to Imagine Possibility

Not certainty. Not guaranteed outcomes. Just possibility.

"Maybe this will get better." "Maybe I'll find a way through." "Maybe there's something I haven't thought of yet."

Hope lives in the maybe. It doesn't demand answers, it simply opens the door.

Realistic hope is a quiet, steady force. It doesn't shout. It doesn't sparkle. But it sustains. It helps you keep going when everything in you wants to give up. It's not about pretending things are easy, it's about believing they're possible.

Closing: The Balance of Positivity

Positivity is not about denying reality. It's about choosing how you respond to it.

It's about:

Acknowledging pain without drowning in it

Practicing gratitude without bypassing grief

Celebrating progress without demanding perfection

Picking your battles to preserve your peace

Reframing your stories to see possibility

Maintaining hope without guaranteeing outcomes

This is the balance we're seeking—the both/and of emotional health:

You can be struggling and grateful

You can be hurting and hopeful

You can feel pain and still choose your response

You are allowed:

To not be positive all the time

To feel what you feel

To have hard days

To celebrate small wins

To let things go

To hope

Positivity isn't a mask, it's a mindset. It's not about pretending life is easy. It's about staying open to the possibility that, even in difficulty, there is still beauty, still meaning, still movement forward.

"Life will break your heart. But it will also fill it. Your job is to stay open to both."

You don't have to do it perfectly. You just have to keep showing up: with honesty, with compassion, and with hope.

You've learned to manage stress, care for yourself, connect with others, and maintain perspective. Now, let's bring it all together because this isn't about perfection. It's about the journey forward.

- Where have I been practicing toxic positivity—either on myself or others?
- What am I genuinely grateful for today, even if today was hard?
- What small win can I celebrate from this week?
- What battle am I fighting that I could let go of?
- What negative story am I telling myself that needs reframing?
- Where do I need more hope? What's one small action I can take?
- How can I balance acknowledging pain with looking for possibility?

Instruction: Choose one or two questions. Write honestly. Remember: positivity isn't about feeling good all the time, it's about choosing perspective when you can, and being gentle with yourself when you can't.

Daily Gratitude Practice

Instructions: Each day, write 3-5 things you're grateful for. Be specific. Include small things. On hard days, it's okay if your gratitude is simple: "I'm grateful I got through today."

Date: _____

Today I'm grateful for:

1.

2.

3.

4.

5.

One small win I'm celebrating today:

One thing that was hard (honoring reality):

One thing I'm looking forward to:

Weekly Reflection (Optional)

This week, I noticed:

A pattern of gratitude (what keeps showing up?):

Something I want to remember:

Gratitude turns what we have into enough.
(Aesop)

Sample Gratitude Journal Entry

Date: Tuesday, March 12

Today I'm grateful for:

My daughter made me laugh when she told me about her day at school. She has her grandmother's sense of humor.

The sun was out for the first time in a week. I sat by the window with my coffee and just felt warm.

My friend texted to check in. I didn't even respond yet, but knowing someone was thinking of me mattered.

My body carried me through a hard workout. I'm tired, but I also feel strong.

Clean sheets. Such a small thing, but climbing into bed tonight felt like a gift.

One small win I'm celebrating today:

I set a boundary with a coworker who keeps dumping extra work on me. I was nervous, but I did it.

One thing that was hard (honoring reality):

I'm worried about money. The car needs repairs and I'm not sure how we'll cover it.

One thing I'm looking forward to:

Coffee with Sarah on Saturday. I need that connection.

Note to readers: Your entries don't have to be this detailed. Some days, "I'm grateful I survived today" is enough. There's no right way to do this. Just show up and notice what you can.

The Journey Forward

It's never too late to be what you might have been. (Attributed to Eliot)

You've reached the end of this book but not the end of your journey.

You've explored strategies, tools, and frameworks. You've reflected on your stress, your habits, your relationships, and your mindset. You've gathered insight. But knowing isn't the same as doing. And now, as you close these pages, you might feel both hopeful and overwhelmed. You might be thinking, "This all makes sense. But how do I actually live it?"

That's a good question. And this chapter isn't here to give you a perfect answer. This is not a flawless 10-step plan to stress-free living. That doesn't exist. This is not a demand that you try everything immediately. That's not sustainable.

This is an invitation to begin, imperfectly, gradually, and with compassion. This is a reminder that transformation happens in small steps, not giant leaps.

The truth about change is that it's not linear. It's messy. It's cyclical. It's deeply human. You'll have good days and hard days. You'll remember these principles and forget them. You'll practice these tools and then neglect them. That's not failure. That's life.

The journey forward isn't about perfecting, it's about returning. Again, and again.

And here's what you've already done: You picked up this book. You read it, or you're reading it now. You've paused to reflect on your life, your stress, your patterns.

You've already begun and that matters.

So, let's talk about what comes next, not as a prescription, but as a companion for the road ahead.

Reviewing the Journey

Before we look forward, let's look back at where we've been.

You've explored what stress is and where it comes from. You've learned to recognize its symptoms, not as signs of failure, but as information. You've discovered how to reframe your stressors, identify your Main Thing, and sort what deserves your energy from what doesn't.

You've given yourself permission to care for yourself. You've explored boundaries, asked for help, and practiced presence through mindfulness and prayer. You've connected your mental health to your physical body: nourishment, movement, sleep. You've reached outward to the people who sustain you. And you've learned to balance genuine positivity with honest acknowledgment of pain.

What connects all of this? Five threads woven through every chapter:

Self-awareness – the courage to notice what's happening

Self-compassion – the grace to be kind to yourself in the process

Agency – the strength to recognize what you can control

Connection – the reminder that you're not alone

Hope – the belief that change is possible

These aren't separate ideas. They're interwoven. Self-awareness opens the door to compassion. Compassion fuels your sense of agency. Agency leads you to seek connection. And connection sustains your hope. This is the through-line. This is the work. And this is the way forward.

Where to Begin

You've learned a lot. Now what? Let's talk about how to start.

Start Where You Are

Here's the truth: you don't need to be ready. You just need to begin. That might sound simple, but it's not always easy. Starting is often the hardest part, not because you're lazy or unmotivated, but because life is messy. Stress is real. And change feels big.

Perhaps hear these thoughts echoing in your mind:

"I'll start when things calm down."

But life rarely calms down on its own. Waiting for the perfect moment is like waiting for a quiet storm. It doesn't come. Start now, in the middle of the mess.

"I need to do all of it perfectly."

Perfection is a trap. You don't need to do everything. You don't need to do it flawlessly. You just need to do something, imperfectly, consistently.

"I don't know which thing to focus on first."

That's okay. Pick one. Any one. The act of choosing is more important than choosing the "right" thing.

"What if I fail?"

You will stumble. You'll forget. You'll fall back into old habits. That's not failure, it's part of the process. Progress isn't a straight line. It's a spiral. You return, again and again.

Here's what I know to be real: There's no perfect time to begin, there's no perfect way to do this, you will make mistakes, you will forget and have to remember again, and that's not a flaw, it's a feature of being human.

Let me tell you a story.

A good friend kept putting off commitment. He wanted to finish his degree first. Get more financially stable. Get in better shape. But every time he tried, life got in the way. Years passed. After losing his brother, something shifted. He realized: the right time isn't coming. The right time is now. So, he called the one person from his past who mattered most. One 10-minute phone call. That was it. He's been married to her for 15 years now. It didn't start big. It started real.

The One Thing Principle

Here's a principle that can change everything: Don't try to change everything at once.

You learned this in Chapter 7, when we talked about habits. But it applies to every part of this book. Stress management, self-care, boundaries, mindfulness, connection, it's all easier when you start with one thing.

So, here's your invitation:

Pick one thing to focus on for the next 2–4 weeks.

Maybe it's setting one boundary, starting a gratitude practice, taking a 10-minute walk each morning, calling a friend weekly, or practicing breath work before bed. Maybe it's finally identifying your Main Thing or asking for help with one specific struggle. Choose one. Any one.

The key is to master one before adding another. Build slowly. Build sustainably.

Why does this work? It prevents overwhelm, you're not juggling everything at once. It creates momentum, small wins lead to bigger ones. It builds confidence, you see that change is possible. And it makes change feel doable, because it is.

This is how real transformation happens. Not in a rush. Not in a frenzy. But in small, intentional steps.

The Priority Matrix: What Needs Attention First?

Not everything needs equal attention. Some things are urgent. Some things are important. Some things are just loud. So how do you decide where to begin?

Here's a simple framework to help you choose your starting point with intention, not pressure.

Ask yourself:

1. What's causing the most pain right now?

Start with what's loudest in your life. Is it physical discomfort, poor sleep, low energy, tension? Is it emotional overwhelm, feeling stretched thin, disconnected, anxious? Is it mental fog, unclear priorities, scattered focus, decision fatigue?

If your body is screaming for rest or nourishment, start there. If your emotions are running high, look at boundaries or mindfulness. If your mind feels cluttered, revisit your "Main Thing."

Pain is a signal. Listen to it.

2. What feels most within my control?

Don't start with the hardest thing. Start with something you can actually influence today. You might not be able to fix your job stress overnight, but you *can* take a walk at lunch. You might not be able to resolve a relationship conflict immediately, but you *can* set one small boundary.

Start where you have agency. Build wins. Create momentum.

3. What would create the most relief?

Sometimes one small change ripples outward. Better sleep creates a better mood, leading to better food choices. One boundary leads to less resentment and better relationships.

Ask yourself: *What's one thing that, if it improved, would make everything else easier?*

4. What excites me (even a little)?

Motivation matters. If something sparks even a little interest, follow that spark. If gratitude feels grounding, start there. If movement feels energizing, start there. If journaling feels clarifying, start there.

You don't need to feel *ready*. You just need to feel *willing*.

Example:

Someone realizes, *"I'm exhausted all the time. My sleep is terrible. That's affecting everything else."* They decide to start with sleep hygiene: a consistent bedtime, a screen-free wind-down routine, and a darker, quieter sleep environment. Within two weeks, their mood improves. Their energy returns. Suddenly, eating better and setting boundaries doesn't feel so impossible. It all started with one choice.

This matrix isn't a checklist, it's a compass. Let it guide you toward the change that matters most *right now*. And remember wherever you begin is the right place to start.

Building Your Plan

You don't need a perfect plan. But a little structure helps. Let's create a simple roadmap.

You've done the reflection. You've chosen where to begin. Now it's time to build a plan that feels doable, not rigid, not overwhelming, but supportive.

Here's a gentle rhythm for your first 30 days. In **week one**, choose one area to focus on, not to change yet, just to notice. Journal your observations. What's happening? How do you feel? This week is about tuning in. In **week two**, choose one small habit related to your focus area and practice it daily (or as often as feels manageable). In **week three**, adjust based on what you've learned. If something's working, keep it. If not, modify it. By **week four**, reflect: What changed? What felt good? Then decide whether to deepen this habit or add something new.

Example Progression:

Week 1: You notice your sleep patterns. You realize you're going to bed at wildly different times.

Week 2: You set a bedtime alarm. You aim to be in bed by 10:30pm most nights.

Week 3: You adjust—10:30 feels too early. You shift to 11pm and add a 20-minute wind-down routine.

Week 4: You feel more rested. Your mood improves. You decide to add morning movement next month.

This plan isn't about fixing your life in 30 days. It's about starting a rhythm of care. It's about showing up for yourself, one week, one habit, one choice at a time.

The "If This, Then That" Tool

Life will throw curveballs. That's not a possibility, it's a guarantee. So instead of hoping everything goes smoothly, let's plan for the bumps. This tool is simple but powerful: Create "if-then" statements, pre-planned responses for when things get hard. They help you stay grounded, compassionate, and intentional when stress hits.

For example, you might think, "If I'm overwhelmed and don't know where to start, then I'll use the 5-4-3-2-1 grounding exercise from Chapter 6." Or "If I'm tempted to skip self-care because I'm "too busy," then I'll remind myself: I can't pour from an empty cup." Or "If I feel isolated and alone, then I'll text one person from my inner circles."

These statements aren't rules as much as they are reminders. They're your lifelines when your nervous system is flooded, when your habits slip, when your inner critic gets loud.

Now it's your turn.

Take a moment to write your own "if-then" statements. Think about the stress patterns you've noticed. The moments you tend to struggle. The thoughts that trip you up. Then ask: What would help me in that moment? What truth do I want to remember? These become your personal guideposts, your way of returning to center when life pulls you off track.

When You Stumble (And You Will)

You will have setbacks. That's not failure, it's part of the process. Let's talk about how to handle them. Setbacks Are Not Failures

Let's bust a myth right now: Slipping up doesn't mean you've failed. It means you're human. We've been taught to think that progress should be clean and linear. That once we start, we should keep going without missing a beat. But that's not how real change works.

Real progress looks more like a squiggly line than a straight arrow. It loops. It dips. It pauses. It climbs. And that's okay.

Here's how to reframe setbacks. Don't tell yourself, "I skipped my habit for three days. I've ruined everything." Instead, say, "I got off track. I can start again today."

You will miss days, forget tools, fall back into old patterns, and feel discouraged. And then you will remember, try again, use a tool, and keep going. That's not failure. That's the journey.

Self-Compassion in Setbacks

When you stumble, and you will, how you talk to yourself matters more than you think.

Harsh self-talk might sound like this: "I'm so weak." "I can't do anything right." "Why do I even try?"

But that voice doesn't help you grow. It shuts you down.

Compassionate self-talk sounds different: "I'm human. This is hard." "I did my best today. Tomorrow is another chance." "I'm learning. Progress isn't linear."

Dr. Kristin Neff's self-compassion framework offers a powerful way to respond to setbacks:

1. **Mindfulness**: Acknowledge what happened without exaggeration.

   "I didn't practice gratitude this week."

2. **Common Humanity:** Remind yourself this is part of being human.

   "Everyone struggles with consistency. I'm not alone in this."

3. **Self-Kindness**: Speak to yourself as you would a friend.

   "It's okay. You can start again tomorrow."

Here's a story:

Someone started a morning meditation practice. For 10 days, they were consistent. They felt calmer, more focused. Then they got sick. Missed a week. Felt like a failure. But instead of giving up, they paused. They reminded themselves: *"I did it for 10 days. I can do it again. One day at a time."* And they returned—not perfectly, but with compassion.

That's the practice.

Returning, Not Starting Over

Here's something important to remember: You're never back at square one.

Every time you practice, even once, you're building something. You're strengthening neural pathways, you're gathering evidence of your capability, and you're learning what works and what doesn't.

So, when you return after a break, you're not starting from scratch. You're returning with experience.

My wife reminds me of this all the time. Just because she hasn't been able to run for a little while, she hasn't lost the skill. In fact, there is this concept of "muscle memory" where your body remembers the movements. Her body might be a little sore, but the groove is still there!

It's the same with these practices. You may forget to journal for a month. You might skip breath work for a week. You might fall out of your gratitude routine. But when you come back, it's easier than the first time. Because you've been there before. You've laid the groundwork.

The practice is in the returning. That's where the growth lives. That's where resilience is built.

The Long View

This isn't about the next 30 days. It's about the rest of your life. Let's zoom out.

Life Will Keep Happening

Here's the truth: life doesn't pause just because you're trying to grow.

New stressors will emerge. Relationships will shift. Jobs will change. Loss will come. And life will surprise you, sometimes in beautiful ways, sometimes in heartbreaking ones.

The tools you've learned in this book won't make you immune to hardship. They're not armor. They're a compass.

You will still feel stressed sometimes, have hard days, struggle with old patterns, and face situations that overwhelm you.

But now, you'll also have tools to manage stress, know how to ask for help, recognize your symptoms earlier, return to your practices more quickly, and trust that you can handle hard things.

The goal was never to eliminate stress. **The goal is resilience.**

Resilience doesn't mean you never fall. It means you know how to get back up. It means you trust yourself to navigate the storm, not avoid it.

Checking In Over Time

Growth isn't a one-time event, it's a lifelong rhythm. And just like any journey, it helps to pause now and then, look around, and ask: *How am I doing?*

Every few months, take time to check in with yourself. These reflections aren't about judgment, they're about recalibration.

Quarterly Reflection Questions:

- What's working? What needs attention?

- Which practices have I sustained? Which have I dropped?

- What's my *Main Thing* right now? (It may have shifted and that's okay.)

- Where do I need support?

- What am I grateful for?

- What do I want to focus on next?

These questions help you stay aligned with what matters most. They help you notice when you're drifting and gently guide you back.

Once a year, go deeper. Reflect on the bigger picture.

Annual Reflection Questions:

- How have I grown this year?

- What did I learn about myself?

- What relationships deepened or changed?

- What habits stuck?

- What's one thing I'm proud of?

- What do I want more of next year?

These check-ins aren't about perfection. They're about presence. They help you honor your progress and set your intention for what's ahead.

Recommitting When Needed

You will need to recommit over and over again. That's not failure. That's the practice. Some seasons, you'll be consistent. Other seasons, you'll barely hold on.

Both are okay.

Recommitment might sound like this: "I drifted. I'm coming back." "Things got hard. I stopped practicing. I'm starting again." "I forgot what mattered. I'm remembering now."

Here's your permission: **You are allowed to restart as many times as you need.** Every return is a victory. Every recommitment is a step forward. And every time you choose to care for yourself again, you're building resilience.

You Are Not Alone on This Journey

You are not the only one struggling with stress, learning boundaries, building healthy habits, or choosing hope. Millions of people are on this same journey, waking up each day, trying to care for themselves, trying to grow. Maybe you feel alone sometimes, but you're not. Every time you choose compassion over criticism, every time you reach out or return to your practices, you join a quiet, powerful movement of people choosing resilience.

This book is a starting point, not an ending. Join a support group. Find a therapist. Connect with others doing this work. Share what you're learning with trusted friends. Revisit chapters when you need a reminder. You don't have to do this alone.

And when you're ready, pass it forward. Not as an expert, but as someone walking the path. Share a tool with a struggling friend. Model boundaries for your kids. Offer to listen. Your healing can become part of someone else's healing. That's how change ripples outward.

Closing: The Invitation

You opened this book because something needed to change. Maybe you were overwhelmed. Maybe you were exhausted. Maybe you just knew, deep down, that you couldn't keep going the way you were going.

And now, you've learned how to understand your stress, how to care for yourself, how to connect with others, and how to maintain perspective and hope. But learning isn't the same as living.

So, here's the invitation: **Live it.** Imperfectly. Gradually. Courageously.

You don't need to be perfect. You just need to be willing, willing to try, to stumble, to return. Willing to believe that small changes matter and that you're capable of more than you know. Willing to hope, even when it's hard.

This journey doesn't end when you close this book. It's just beginning.

Because that's what resilience is: **Not the absence of struggle. But the courage to keep showing up anyway.**

So here are my final words to you:

You are not broken. You are not failing. You are not too much or not enough. You are human. And being human is hard.

But you are also capable. You are resilient. You are worthy of care, connection, and hope. You've got this. Not because it will be easy. But because you are stronger than you know.

One step. One breath. One day at a time. That's the journey forward. And I'm cheering for you.

FINAL REFLECTION: YOUR COMMITMENT TO YOURSELF

Instructions: Take a few minutes to write a letter to your future self. This letter is your anchor—something you can return to when things get hard, when you forget why you started, or when you need a reminder of your commitment.

Dear Future Me,

Right now, I'm reading this book because:

The main thing I want to change in my life is:

My Main Thing (from Chapter 4) is:

One practice I commit to starting is:

When I stumble or forget, I will remind myself:

I am doing this because:

I believe I am capable of:

One year from now, I hope to:

Sign and date this letter. Keep it somewhere you'll see it.

Answer these questions to clarify your starting point:

1. What ONE thing will I focus on for the next 30 days?

☐ Sleep routine

☐ Daily gratitude

☐ Movement practice

☐ Setting one boundary

☐ Connecting with inner circle

☐ Mindfulness practice

☐ Identifying my Main Thing

☐ Other: _____

2. What will this look like specifically?

Example: "I will go to bed by 11pm at least 5 nights a week."

My specific commitment:

3. Who will support me in this?

Name one person I can share this commitment with:

4. How will I know if it's working?

What will be different after 30 days?

5. My "if-then" plan for obstacles:

If _____ happens, then I will _____

If _____ happens, then I will _____

If _____ happens, then I will _____

Resources for Continued Growth

Books mentioned or referenced:

- *Man's Search for Meaning* by Viktor Frankl

- *Atomic Habits* by James Clear

- *The Artist's Way* by Julia Cameron

- Self-compassion work by Dr. Kristin Neff

Organizations and resources:

- NAMI (National Alliance on Mental Illness): nami.org

- Psychology Today therapist directory

- Open Path Collective (affordable therapy)

- Local support groups (see Chapter 8)

Emergency resources:

- National Suicide Prevention Lifeline: 988

- Crisis Text Line: Text HOME to 741741

- SAMHSA National Helpline: 1-800-662-4357

Final Blessing

May you be gentle with yourself.

May you remember that progress is not linear.

May you find courage in small steps.

May you know you are not alone.

May you return to these practices as often as you need.

May you extend to yourself the same compassion you offer
others.

May you trust that you are exactly where you need to be.

May you keep going—one breath, one day, one step at a time.

The journey forward is yours.

And it begins now.

THE END

(Or, more accurately: **THE BEGINNING**)

Works Cited

BOOKS

Cameron, Julia. The Artist's Way: A Spiritual Path to Higher Creativity. TarcherPerigee, 1992.

Clear, James. Atomic Habits: An Easy & Proven Way to Build Good Habits & Break Bad Ones. Avery, 2018.

Coles, Robert. The Call of Stories: Teaching and the Moral Imagination. Houghton Mifflin, 1989.

Covey, Stephen R. The 7 Habits of Highly Effective People: Powerful Lessons in Personal Change. Free Press, 1989.

Covey, Stephen R. First Things First. Simon & Schuster, 1994.

Dyer, Wayne. Your Erroneous Zones. Funk & Wagnalls, 1976.

Frankl, Viktor E. Man's Search for Meaning. Beacon Press, 2006. (Original work published 1946)

Keller, Helen. Optimism: An Essay. T.Y. Crowell & Company, 1903.

Kushner, Harold S. When Bad Things Happen to Good People. Anchor Books, 1981.

Lorde, Audre. A Burst of Light and Other Essays. Firebrand Books, 1988.

Mackesy, Charlie. The Boy, the Mole, the Fox and the Horse. HarperOne, 2019.

Selye, Hans. The Stress of Life. McGraw-Hill, 1978. (Revised edition; original work published 1956)

ARTICLES & RESEARCH

DeLongis, Anita, Susan Folkman, and Richard S. Lazarus. "The Impact of Daily Stress on Health and Mood: Psychological and Social Resources as Mediators." *Journal of Personality and Social Psychology* 54, no. 3 (1988): 486-495.

Gillespie, Lane. "Survey: 43% of Americans say money is negatively impacting their mental health." Bankrate, April 30, 2025. https://www.bankrate.com/banking/money-and-mental-health-survey/.

Hamilton, Odessa S., Eleonora Iob, Olesya Ajnakina, James B. Kirkbride, and Andrew Steptoe. "Immune-neuroendocrine patterning and response to stress: A latent profile analysis in the English longitudinal study of ageing." *Brain, Behavior, and Immunity* 115 (2024): 600-608. https://doi.org/10.1016/j.bbi.2023.11.012.

Holmes, Thomas H., and Richard H. Rahe. "The Social Readjustment Rating Scale." *Journal of Psychosomatic Research* 11, no. 2 (1967): 213-218.

Skapinakis, P., S. Weich, G. Lewis, et al. "Socio-economic position and common mental disorders: Longitudinal study in the general population in the UK." *British Journal of Psychiatry* 189 (2006): 109-117.

Valtorta, Nicole K., Mona Kanaan, Simon Gilbody, Sara Ronzi, and Barbara Hanratty. "Loneliness and social isolation as risk factors for coronary heart disease and stroke: systematic review and meta-analysis of longitudinal observational studies." *Heart* 102, no. 13 (2016): 1009-1016. doi: 10.1136/heartjnl-2015-308790.

Williamson, A.M., and A.M. Feyer. "Moderate sleep deprivation produces impairments in cognitive and motor performance equivalent to legally prescribed levels of alcohol intoxication." *Occupational and Environmental Medicine* 57 (2000): 649-655.

CLASSICAL SOURCES

Juvenal. Satires. Circa 100 AD. (Source of Latin phrase mens sana in corpore sano)

TRADITIONAL & ATTRIBUTED QUOTES

Attributed Quotes:

Arthur Ashe: "Start where you are. Use what you have. Do what you can."

Dalai Lama: "Sleep is the best meditation."

George Eliot (Mary Ann Evans): "It's never too late to be what you might have been." (Commonly attributed; disputed origin)

Jim Rohn: "Take care of your body. It's the only place you have to live."

Reinhold Niebuhr: "Serenity Prayer" (circa 1932-1943)

Thích Nhất Hạnh: "The present moment is the only time over which we have dominion."

Zen proverb: "You should sit in meditation for twenty minutes every day—unless you're too busy. Then you should sit for an hour."

ORGANIZATIONS & RESOURCES

Mental Health & Support Organizations:

DBSA (Depression and Bipolar Support Alliance): www.dbsalliance.org

GriefShare: www.griefshare.org

MOPS (Mothers of Preschoolers): www.mops.org

NAMI (National Alliance on Mental Illness): www.nami.org

Psychology Today Support Group Directory: www.psychologytoday.com

The Dinner Party (grief support): www.thedinnerparty.org

Assessment Tools:

Holmes-Rahe Life Stress Inventory: www.stress.org

The Hassles and Uplifts Scale (DeLongis, Folkman, & Lazarus, 1982)

THERAPEUTIC APPROACHES REFERENCED

ACT (Acceptance and Commitment Therapy)

CBT-I (Cognitive Behavioral Therapy for Insomnia)

DBT (Dialectical Behavior Therapy)

MBSR (Mindfulness-Based Stress Reduction) - developed by Jon Kabat-Zinn

REBT (Rational Emotive Behavior Therapy) - developed by Albert Ellis

NOTES ON SOURCES

General Medical/Health Knowledge:

Many facts cited in this book (brain composition, sleep recommendations, caffeine metabolism, etc.) are established medical knowledge drawn from general health science education and are not attributed to specific sources.

Quote Authenticity:

Some widely circulated quotes have uncertain or disputed origins. Where applicable, these are noted as "attributed to" or "commonly attributed to" the named source.

For additional reading recommendations, see the "Further Reading" section at the end of this book.

Further Reading

STRESS, BURNOUT, AND RESILIENCE

Unstressable – Mo Gawdat & Alice Law

Stress Tested – Dr. Richard Mackenzie & Peter Walker

The Stress-Proof Brain – Melanie Greenberg

The Stress Solution – Dr. Rangan Chatterjee

Burnout: The Secret to Unlocking the Stress Cycle – Emily & Amelia Nagoski

The Stress Prescription – Dr. Elissa Epel

The 5 Resets – Dr. Aditi Nerurkar

Building a Non-Anxious Life – Dr. John Delony

The Upside of Stress – Kelly McGonigal

Burnout Immunity – Kandi Wiens

The Myth of Normal – Gabor Maté

Atlas of the Heart – Brené Brown

Emotional Agility – Susan David

MINDFULNESS AND EMOTIONAL WELL-BEING

Wherever You Go, There You Are – Jon Kabat-Zinn

Full Catastrophe Living – Jon Kabat-Zinn

The Happiness Trap – Russ Harris

Mindfulness for Stress Management – Catherine Polan Orzech

That Little Voice in Your Head – Mo Gawdat

Real Happiness – Sharon Salzberg

The Mindful Path to Self-Compassion – Christopher Germer

10% Happier – Dan Harris

The Body Keeps the Score – Bessel van der Kolk

Radical Acceptance – Tara Brach

COGNITIVE AND BEHAVIORAL STRATEGIES

Why Has Nobody Told Me This Before? – Dr. Julie Smith

Stop Overthinking – Nick Trenton

Don't Sweat the Small Stuff – Richard Carlson

The Anxiety and Phobia Workbook – Edmund J. Bourne

The Strengths-Based Workbook for Stress Relief – Ryan M. Niemiec

Cleaning Up Your Mental Mess – Dr. Caroline Leaf

Stop Letting Everything Affect You – Daniel Chidiac

Thinking, Fast and Slow – Daniel Kahneman

Feeling Good: The New Mood Therapy – David Burns

The CBT Toolbox – Jeff Riggenbach

SELF-CARE AND HEALTHY HABITS

The Self-Care Prescription – Dr. Robyn Gobin

How to Keep House While Drowning – KC Davis

Mommy Burnout – Dr. Sheryl Ziegler

Help in a Hurry – Dr. Caroline Leaf

101 Ways to Be Less Stressed – Dr. Caroline Leaf

The Four Tendencies – Gretchen Rubin

Rest: Why You Get More Done When You Work Less – Alex Soojung-Kim Pang

Why We Sleep – Matthew Walker

The Joy of Movement – Kelly McGonigal

CONNECTION, COMMUNITY, AND SUPPORT

Together: The Healing Power of Human Connection – Vivek Murthy

The Gifts of Imperfection – Brené Brown

Daring Greatly – Brené Brown

Further Engagement

If something in this book sparks a memory or story from your own life, I'd love to hear from you. With your permission, I may share your story anonymously to help others on their journey.

Through my agency, Performance+, I offer workshops and consulting services in stress management, resilience building, leadership development, and organizational culture. My approach blends research-based strategies with interactive exercises and practical application—creating meaningful change that participants can implement immediately.

If you're interested in bringing a workshop to your organization, school, or team, or would like to discuss how Performance+ can support your group's growth, please reach out. I'd be happy to explore how we can tailor content to your specific needs.

Performance+
www.myperformanceplus.org

Malcolm Eric Meadows
eric@myperformanceplus.org